RANGE

How Exploring
Your Interests Can Change the
World

ALSO BY DAVID EPSTEIN

The Sports Gene

RANGE

How Exploring Your Interests Can Change the **World**

Adapted for Young Readers

by David Epstein

Adapted by Catherine S. Frank

VIKING

VIKING
An imprint of Penguin Random House LLC
1745 Broadway, New York, New York 10019

First published in the United States of America by Viking, an imprint of Penguin Random House LLC, 2025

Text copyright © 2025 by David Epstein
Illustrations copyright © 2025 by Berat Pekmezci

Visit us online at PenguinRandomHouse.com.

Library of Congress Cataloging-in-Publication Data is available.

ISBN 9780593624036
2nd Printing

Manufactured in the United States of America
BVG

Edited by Kelsey Murphy
Design by Anabeth Bostrup
Text set in Acta Book

The authorized representative in the EU for product safety and compliance is Penguin Random House Ireland,
Morrison Chambers, 32 Nassau Street, Dublin D02 YH68, Ireland, https://eu-contact.penguin.ie.

For Andre,
my very own young reader

Contents

Introduction

Team Tiger or Team Roger?

Legendary golf player Tiger Woods and tennis icon Roger Federer did not meet each other until 2006, when both athletes were at the height of their powers. Woods attended the final of the US Open tennis tournament in New York, in which Federer was playing. Knowing Woods was there made Federer especially nervous, but he still won, for the third year in a row. Woods joined him in the locker room to celebrate. They connected as only two athletes with their level of stardom could and quickly became friends.

"I've never spoken with anybody who was so familiar with the feeling of being invincible," Federer would later say of his friendship with Woods. Still, their connection almost seemed to surprise him. "Even as a kid his goal was to break the record for winning the most majors. I was just dreaming of just once meeting Boris Becker or being able to play at Wimbledon sometime," Federer told a biographer. "His story is completely different from mine."

Federer was right. The origin story of Tiger Woods and his legendary golfing career is remarkable, and it has proved to be highly influential.

When Tiger was just a baby, his father could tell something

was different about his son. At six months old, the boy could balance on his father's hand as his father walked through their home. When Tiger was seven months old, his father gave him a golf club to fool around with, and Tiger dragged it everywhere with him. At ten months old, he climbed down from his high chair, toddled over to a golf club that had been cut down to be the right size for him, and imitated his father's swing, which he'd been watching in the garage. Tiger was so young he couldn't talk yet, so his father drew pictures to show him how to correctly place his hands on the club. "It is very difficult to communicate how to putt when the child is too young to talk," his father would later note.

At age two—when most children are reaching typical developmental milestones like kicking a ball and standing on tiptoe—Tiger hit a ball on national television using a golf club that was tall enough to reach his shoulder. That same year, he entered his first golf tournament and won the ten-and-under division. At two! His father decided there was no time to waste. By age three, Tiger was learning how to hit his ball out of the sand traps found on golf courses (he called them "sand twaps"), and his father was mapping out his destiny. He knew his son had been chosen for golf greatness and that it was his duty to guide him.

He felt so certain about Tiger's path that he started teaching his three-year-old how to talk to the media. Pretending to be a reporter, he quizzed Tiger, teaching him how to give brief answers and never to offer more than precisely what was asked.

When Tiger was four, his father could drop him off at a golf course at nine in the morning and pick him up eight hours later. Sometimes Tiger came home with money he'd won from those foolish enough to doubt his abilities.

At age eight, Tiger beat his father for the first time. Tiger's father didn't mind, because he was convinced that his son was singularly talented and that he was uniquely equipped to help him. He had been an outstanding athlete himself, against enormous odds. Tiger's father had played baseball in college, and he was the only Black player in the entire conference at the time. He understood people, and discipline. He knew he hadn't done his best with three kids from a previous marriage, but now he could see that he'd been given a second chance to do the right thing with Tiger. And it was all going according to plan.

Tiger was famous by the time he reached college, and soon his father began talking about his importance in history. His son would have a larger impact than legendary world leaders like Nelson Mandela and Mohandas Gandhi, even greater than the Buddha, he insisted: "There is no limit because he has the guidance. I don't know yet exactly what form this will take. But he is the Chosen One."

Tiger's story of becoming an elite golfer is incredible and, as Roger Federer himself noted, completely different from the way Roger's own story of becoming a tennis champion played out.

Roger's mom was a coach, but she never coached him. He would kick a ball around with her after he learned to walk. And as a young boy, he played squash with his father on Sundays. He also dabbled in skiing, wrestling, swimming, and skateboarding. He played basketball, handball, tennis, table tennis, badminton over his neighbor's fence, and soccer at school. He would later give credit to the wide range of sports he played for helping him develop his athleticism and hand-eye coordination.

Roger found that which sport he was playing really didn't matter much to him, so long as it included a ball. "I was always very much more interested if a ball was involved," he would later remember. He was a kid who loved to play. His parents had no particular athletic aspirations for him. "We had no plan A, no plan B," his mother said. She and Roger's father encouraged him to sample a wide range of sports. In fact, playing many sports was essential because it kept him busy. Roger "became unbearable," his mother said, if he had to stay still for too long.

Though his mother taught tennis, she decided against working with him. "He would have just upset me anyway," she said. "He tried out every strange stroke and certainly never returned a ball normally. That is simply no fun for a mother."

When he was almost a teenager, Roger began to lean more toward tennis, and if his parents "nudged him at all, it was to stop taking tennis so seriously." When Roger played matches, his mother often wandered away to chat with friends instead of watching every point. His father had only one rule: "Just don't cheat." Roger didn't, and he started getting really good.

Roger was competitive, no doubt. But when his tennis instructors decided to move him up to a group with older players, he asked to move back so he could stay with his friends. After all, part of the fun was hanging around after his lessons to talk about music, or pro wrestling, or soccer.

By the time Roger finally gave up other sports—soccer, most notably—to focus on tennis, other players he faced had long since been working with strength coaches, sports psychologists, and nutritionists. To some, it may have looked like he was behind in his training. But it didn't seem to get in the way of his development in the long run. When Roger was in his mid-thirties, which is when many professional tennis players have typically retired, he was still ranked number one in the world.

It may seem pretty unusual for a kid like Roger, who took his sport lightly at first, to grow into a dominant champion like no one before him. Thousands of tennis players, if not more, had a head start on Roger. His was an entirely different scenario from that of Tiger, whose incredible upbringing has been the focus of bestselling books about how to develop expertise. Tiger was not merely playing golf. He was engaging in what is known as "deliberate practice," the only kind that matters to expertise, according to a concept known as the ten-thousand-hours rule. The ten-thousand-hours idea basically says that in order to develop a skill and become an expert at it, the only thing that matters is the number of hours you devote to practicing it, no matter what the skill may be. There is a lot of data about how athletes reach the elite level, and it shows that those athletes spend more time on high-level, deliberate practice each week than athletes who never reach the elite level.

Tiger and his origin story have come to symbolize this idea that the amount of deliberate practice devoted to an activity is what determines success and, therefore, that deliberate practice must start as early as possible. As the British sports scientist and coach Ian Yates told me, parents increasingly come to him and "want their kids doing what the Olympians are doing right now, not what the Olympians were doing when they were twelve or thirteen." They believe their kids should begin elite-level deliberate practice immediately, similar to how Tiger began.

But that approach from well-meaning parents skips over the fact that what those Olympians were doing when they were twelve or thirteen probably didn't look like Olympic-level deliberate practice. They were probably still trying out a wider variety of activities that developed their general athleticism, like Roger did. That variety would have allowed them to figure out what they really liked and what they were really good at before they focused narrowly on deliberate practice and developing specialized skills. This "sampling period"—a time of trying out many different things—is essential to the development of great performers. It's not something to be skipped in order to get a head start.

When we look at the existing data, the idea of an athlete, even one who wants to become elite, following Roger's path and trying different sports makes a lot of sense. Elite athletes at the peak of their abilities do spend more time on focused, deliberate practice. But those athletes typically devote *less* time early on to the activity in which they will eventually become experts.

In other words, elite athletes don't skip that sampling period. They play a variety of sports. They gain a range of physical skills that improve their athleticism. They learn about their own abilities and preferences. It's only later, after this sampling period, that they focus and start specializing in a single sport. Specializing early obviously worked for Tiger, but according to research, his path is the exception for great athletes and Roger's is the norm.

When I began to write about these studies, I was met with some criticism, and even denial. "Maybe in some other sport," fans often said, "but that's not true of *our* sport." Soccer fans were especially outspoken about this. It's hard to believe that the players on your favorite team haven't always devoted their entire lives to their sport. But then another study came out showing that Germany's 2014 World Cup–winning national team was made up of players who continued playing nonorganized soccer and other sports into their twenties. Other studies show similar findings about late specialization in a wide range of sports, from hockey to volleyball. In reality, the Roger path to sports stardom is far more common than the Tiger path. But those athletes' stories are much more quietly told, if they are told at all.

The push to focus on one skill early and narrowly extends

well beyond sports. We are often told that the more competitive and complicated the world gets, the more specialized we all must become (and the earlier we must start) to navigate it. A 2019 report found that by age seven children significantly narrow their ideas of what they will choose for a career when they grow up. And some of our best-known icons of success are celebrated for their head starts—Mozart playing the piano before he was five; Mark Zuckerberg dropping out of college and cofounding Facebook.

It is certainly true that there are areas that require experts with Tiger-like skills and purpose, especially as the world becomes increasingly complex. But Tiger's uniquely early focus on one specialized skill is not the only path to success. It's not actually the typical path to success. In fact, being open to a wide range of activities and being willing to try new experiences early on in life can lead to becoming an expert later.

There's plenty of evidence that demonstrates why we need more Rogers in the world, more people with range. I hope this book shows the benefits of range and of a Roger-like approach in any area that matters to you, whether it's choosing a sport or hobby, imagining what you may want to study later in life, or anything else you can dream up.

PART 1

Exploration: Figuring It Out

Chess, Anyone?

In May 1946, one year and four days after World War II in Europe ended, Laszlo Polgar was born in a small town in Hungary. His birth was essentially the beginning of a new family. He had no grandmothers, no grandfathers, and no cousins; all of them had been murdered in the Holocaust, along with his father's first wife and five children. Laszlo grew up determined to have a family, and a special one.

As a college student, he was already thinking about becoming a father in the future, and he prepared by reading biographies of legendary thinkers, from Socrates to Albert

Einstein. Laszlo decided that traditional education systems were broken and that he could make his own future children into geniuses if he just gave them the right head start. By doing so, he would prove that any child can be molded for greatness in any discipline. Laszlo also realized he needed a wife who would go along with the plan.

Laszlo's mother had a friend, and the friend had a daughter, Klara. In 1965, Klara traveled to Budapest, where she met Laszlo in person. Laszlo spent their first visit telling Klara that he planned to have six children and that he would nurture them to brilliance. Klara returned home to her parents and gave Laszlo an unenthusiastic review: She had "met a very interesting person" but could not imagine marrying him.

They continued to exchange letters, though. They were both teachers and agreed that the school system was frustratingly one-size-fits-all, made for producing "the gray average mass," as Laszlo put it. A year and a half of letters later, Klara's feelings had changed, and she realized she had a very special pen pal. Laszlo finally proposed to Klara in a love letter. They married, moved to Budapest, and got to work on Laszlo's plan. Their daughter Susan was born in early 1969, and the experiment was on.

To mold and create his first genius, Laszlo picked chess, the ancient game of strategy and cunning. In 1972, the year before Susan started her training, an American chess grandmaster named Bobby Fischer had defeated the Russian player Boris Spassky in a World Chess Championship match, which came to be known as the "Match of the Century." Because of the popularity of that match, suddenly chess was a part of pop culture just about everywhere. Plus, according to Klara, the game had a distinct benefit: "Chess is very objective and easy to measure." You can win, you can lose, or you can have a draw, in which no one wins. And there's a point system to measure skill against the rest of the chess world. His daughter, Laszlo decided, would become a chess champion.

Laszlo was patient and thorough. He started Susan's chess training with "pawn wars," which meant playing the game with only the pawn pieces. The first person to advance to the back row wins. She enjoyed chess and caught on quickly. Soon, Susan was studying more advanced phases of the game and moves, including endgames and opening traps. After eight months, Laszlo took her to a chess club in Budapest and challenged grown men to play his four-year-old daughter, whose legs dangled from her chair. Susan won her first game, and the man she beat stormed off. She entered the Budapest girls' championship and won the under-eleven title. At age four she had not lost a game.

By six years of age, Susan could read and write and was

way ahead of her peers in math. Laszlo and Klara decided they would homeschool her and keep the day open for chess. Susan's new little sister, Sofia, would be homeschooled too, as would Judit, who was coming soon and whom Laszlo and Klara almost named Zseni, which is the Hungarian word for "genius." All three of their daughters became part of the grand experiment.

On a normal day, the girls were at the gym by seven a.m. playing table tennis with trainers and then back home at ten for breakfast before a long day of chess. When Laszlo reached the limit of his own expertise, he hired coaches for his three geniuses in training. He spent his extra time cutting out records of game sequences from chess journals. He filed two hundred thousand game sequences in a custom catalog. Before computer chess programs existed, Laszlo's catalog gave the Polgars the largest known chess database in the world to study.

When Susan was seventeen, she became the first woman to qualify for the men's world championship, but the World Chess Federation did not allow her to participate. That rule would soon be changed thanks to her accomplishments. Two years later, in 1988, when Sofia was fourteen and Judit was twelve, the girls became three of the four Hungarian team members for the Women's Chess Olympiad. They won, beating the Soviet Union, which had won eleven of the twelve Olympiads since the event began.

The Polgar sisters became "national treasures," as Susan put it. The following year, the girls competed all over the world. In January 1991, when she was twenty-one years old, Susan became the first woman to achieve grandmaster status through tournament play against men. ("Grandmaster" is the highest title a player can earn in chess, and once it's achieved, it's kept for life.) That December, Judit, at fifteen years and five months old, became the youngest grandmaster ever, male or female. When Susan was asked on television if she wanted to win the world championship in the men's or women's category, she cleverly responded that she wanted to win the "absolute category."

None of the sisters ultimately reached Laszlo's highest goal of becoming the overall world champion, but all were outstanding players. In 1996, Susan participated in the women's world championship and won. Sofia peaked at the rank of international master, a level down from grandmaster. Judit went furthest, climbing up to eighth in the overall world ranking in 2004.

Laszlo's experiment had worked. In fact, it worked so well that in the early 1990s he suggested that if his early-specialization approach were applied to a thousand children, humanity could tackle problems like curing cancer and AIDS. After all, chess was just the activity he chose for his experiment in early specialization. Like the Tiger Woods origin story, the Polgar story became popular and well known through articles, books, TV shows, and talks. It became an example of the power of an early start, of what might be called a life hack today. An online course called "Bring Up Genius!" advertises lessons in the Polgar method to "build up your own Genius Life Plan."

The powerful idea behind the Polgar method is that anything in the world can be conquered using the same methods. Notice, though, that this lesson relies on one very important and very unspoken assumption: that the way to excel at chess (or golf) is also the way to excel at any other activity that matters to you. And, the fact is, most of the things you probably want to learn and do in life *aren't* like chess and golf.

In 2009, two psychologists named Daniel Kahneman and Gary Klein explored whether or not a lot of specialized experience always leads to expertise. They found that it depends entirely on the activity, or the domain, in question.

In golf or chess, a ball or piece is moved according to rules and within defined boundaries. There are limited options for what can happen. Hit a golf ball, for example, and it either goes too far or not far enough; it either curves through the air or flies straight. The player can observe what happened, attempt to correct any errors, and try again with their next swing. And since similar situations occur over and over again in the same game, a player can know very quickly whether they've corrected their error or made things worse. Feedback in predictable games like golf and chess is extremely accurate and usually very rapid. Your golf ball flies straight or it doesn't. Your knight is captured on the chessboard or it's not. You adjust as needed. This is the very definition of deliberate practice: a learner improves simply by engaging in the activity and immediately correcting their errors.

But in activities or learning environments where the rules are unclear or incomplete, there may not be repetitive patterns and feedback to learn from. And even if there are, they may not be obvious. In some unpredictable situations, relying on previous experience can actually cause problems. For example, it turns out that firefighters who are experts at putting out house fires can't depend on their experience if they're sent to fight a fire in a skyscraper instead. The situations are completely different, so their expertise doesn't apply. In fact, if they rely on experience gained from years of fighting house fires, they are likely to make poor decisions when fighting a skyscraper blaze. It doesn't take much to throw even experienced pros off course.

How a Chess Master Thinks

Garry Kasparov is considered by many to be the greatest chess player in history. When I asked the Russian grandmaster to explain his decision process before he makes a move, he told me, "I see a move, a combination, almost instantly," based on patterns that he has seen many times before. Kasparov said he would bet that grandmasters usually make the move that springs to mind in the first few seconds of thought. It's a clear indication that chess players of the highest level rely on previous experience.

Elite-level chess players have been facing off against computer opponents for decades. As far back as 1997, the Russian grandmaster Garry Kasparov put his natural intelligence to the test against an IBM supercomputer's artificial intelligence (AI). (The computer won.) After that, Kasparov helped organize the first "advanced chess" tournament, in which each human player, including Kasparov himself, was paired with a computer and played against other human-computer duos. The machine would use AI to handle groups of a few moves so the human could focus on big-picture, game-winning strategy. It was like Tiger Woods facing off in a golf video game against the best gamers. Kasparov's years of experience and repetition playing chess were suddenly less useful because supercomputers were involved. "My advantage in calculating tactics had been nullified by the machine," he said. In other words, AI was better at making tactical moves. (In the tournament, Kasparov and his computer partner settled for a 3–3 draw against a human player he'd beaten in a traditional match just a month earlier.)

Eventually, some elite chess players began playing in team tournaments with teams that could be made up of multiple humans and computers. These are known as "freestyle chess" tournaments. In a 2014 tournament, the winning team was made up of four people and several computers. The captain of the team was, at best, a decent chess player. He was certainly not a grandmaster. But he was very good at making real-time strategy decisions. His teammate told me,

"What people don't understand is that freestyle involves an integrated set of skills that in some cases have nothing to do with playing chess." If he were playing traditional chess, the team captain would just be an amateur. But because he knew computers very well and was a strategic leader who listened to his team's advice, he ultimately led them to freestyle-chess victory.

What has all of this competition and partnering between humans and supercomputers shown? What does playing chess against AI teach us about human intelligence? Our greatest strength is the ability to think broadly and strategically. The bigger the picture, the more potential there is for uniquely human contribution.

The progress of AI in the narrow and orderly world of chess has been enormous because instant feedback and bottomless data are available for AI to learn from. But in messier, less predictable environments, there are still challenges with AI. Take AI-driven cars, for example. There's been a lot of progress in the self-driving-car department, but issues remain. And in truly unpredictable, no-rules-apply real-world problems, AI has been disastrous. And that's because there are no rigid rules or perfect data for AI to learn from in the messy real world.

IBM's AI computer system, known as Watson, had success

playing the game show *Jeopardy!* After its victory, it was proposed that Watson could revolutionize cancer care. Unfortunately, the attempt was a flop. In fact, Watson failed so badly that several AI experts told me they worried its reputation would set AI research in health-related fields back. As one doctor put it, "The difference between winning at *Jeopardy!* and curing all cancer is that we know the answer to *Jeopardy!* questions." Watson already had all of the information it needed to win a trivia game show. But, since there is much humans still don't know about cancer, the data that an AI system like Watson needs doesn't exist yet. With cancer, we're still working on posing the right questions in the first place, so Watson can't access the data it needs. It can't learn what isn't yet known.

When humans know the rules and answers and they don't change over time—like in chess, and golf, and playing classical music on an instrument—an argument can be made for pursuing intensely specialized practice from day one. But most of the things that people are interested in learning aren't as predictable as the best way to hit a golf ball or how to play certain musical notes.

As we've seen, the habit of falling back on previous experience can go terribly wrong in some situations—like the firefighters who are experts at putting out house fires, who suddenly make poor choices when faced with a fire in a skyscraper. And this is bad news for someone who wants to rely on some of pop culture's favorite successful-learning examples like the Polgars and Tiger.

Life is not a round of golf or a chess match. Nor is it even tennis. As the psychologist Robin Hogarth put it, much of the world can seem like "Martian tennis." You can see the players on a court with balls and rackets, but nobody has shared the rules with you. It is up to you to figure them out, and they are subject to change without notice.

Tiger's story and the Polgar story give the false impression that human skill is always developed in a predictable learning environment. If that were the case, specialization that is narrow and that begins as soon as possible would usually be successful. But that approach doesn't even work in most sports. We have been using the wrong stories.

There are, of course, areas besides chess and golf in which massive amounts of narrow practice creates experts. Surgeons improve with repetition of the same procedure. And successful accountants as well as bridge and poker players also benefit from repetitive experience.

But when the rules are changed just a little bit, it can seem that experts have traded the ability to be flexible and to adapt for honing their narrow skill. In research about the card game bridge, for example, expert players had a harder time adapting when the order of who played first in each round was changed than nonexperts did. And in a study where experienced accountants were asked to use a new tax law that replaced a previous one, they made more mistakes than new accountants. Research has shown that it's possible to avoid this kind of inflexibility, and one way to do that is by not limiting yourself to one narrow skill. Or, as one researcher put it, to insist on "having one foot outside your world."

Scientists and members of the general public are about equally likely to have artistic hobbies. But it turns out that the more successful scientists, like those who have been inducted into the highest-level national academies, are much more likely to have interests outside of their jobs. And scientists who have won the Nobel Prize are more likely still to pursue other hobbies. Compared to other scientists, Nobel laureates are at least twenty-two times more likely to be an amateur actor, dancer, magician, or other type of performer. Nationally recognized scientists are much more likely than other scientists to be musicians, sculptors, painters, printmakers, woodworkers, mechanics, electronics tinkerers, glassblowers, poets, or writers of both fiction and nonfiction.

This data shows that the most successful experts belong to the wider world outside of their fields of expertise. A years-long study of scientists and engineers, all of whom were true experts, found that those who did not make a creative contribution to their field lacked other interests outside their narrow area. The psychologist and prominent creativity researcher Dean Keith Simonton observed that creative achievers tend to have broad interests "rather than obsessively focus[ing] on a narrow topic."

Apple cofounder Steve Jobs famously recounted the influence of a calligraphy writing class he took on his approach to designing his first computer. "When we were designing the first Macintosh computer, it all came back to me," he said. "If I had never dropped in on that single course in college, the Mac would never" have used the fonts that it did.

Pretending the world is as predictable and neat as a round of golf or a game of chess may be comforting. It makes for a tidy message and for some very compelling books about how to become an expert at something. But the real world is a place with ill-defined challenges and few rigid rules, and where it may often feel like you're being forced to play Martian tennis. And that's why having range really can be a life hack.

QUESTIONS

1. Do you consider yourself an expert at a certain skill or subject? Can you think of any ways you could widen your area of expertise? How could you change things up to expand beyond a narrow focus?

2. Do you think the Polgar sisters could have become excellent chess players without their father's experiment?

3. Are the things you're interested in more like chess, with rules that never change, or do you prefer activities where the rules are less clear?

QUESTIONS

4. Can you think of a time when you learned something more broadly and then chose to narrow your focus later? For example, did you learn and try different positions on a soccer field before choosing to be goalkeeper?

5. Do you worry it's too late to try something new? Or are you open to exploring new interests and skills?

2

Never Settle

When he was a young boy, Vincent van Gogh tried to sketch the family cat. The result was so terrible he destroyed the picture and refused to try again. Instead, he spent his childhood in the Netherlands playing marbles and sledding with his little brother, and mostly just looking at things. He wandered alone for hours. He walked in storms and at night. He walked for miles just to sit for hours watching a bird's nest or following water bugs as they traveled across a brook. He was especially obsessed with collecting beetles, labeling each one with its proper Latin species name. There was little hint in his childhood that he would eventually produce some of the most famous paintings in the world.

In 1866, at age thirteen, Vincent was admitted to a brand-new school located in a hulking former royal palace. It was so far from his home that he had to board with a local family. His mind was elsewhere during class, but he was a good student and spent his free time memorizing poetry.

Vincent didn't like living with strangers, so he left the school just before he turned fifteen. For the next sixteen months, he did little other than take long nature walks. That could not go on forever, but he had no idea what else to do. Fortunately, his uncle owned a successful art dealership, which bought and sold pieces of art. He offered his nephew a job. Vincent accepted, and by the time he was twenty he was dealing with important clients and traveling on sales trips. He confidently told his parents that he would never have to look for a job again. He was wrong.

He was soon transferred to work in a London office that did not deal directly with customers, and then, when he was twenty-two years old, he was transferred again, this time to Paris. He arrived in France at the time of an artistic revolution. On his walks to work, he passed the studios of artists who were in the process of becoming famous. And yet, as a pair of Van Gogh's future biographers would write, "none of it registered." Years later, when he and his little brother discussed those revolutionary Parisian artists, he would say he had "seen absolutely nothing of them."

Eventually Vincent was fired from the art dealership, and he went to work as an assistant teacher at a boarding school in a seaside town in England. He taught classes from French to math, oversaw the dormitory, took the students to church, and acted as the school's handyman. He moved on to another job as a tutor, this time at a fancier boarding school. But after a few months of that, he decided he would become a missionary in South America. His parents talked him out of it. So then he decided to follow in his father's footsteps; he would train to become a pastor.

In the meantime, his father arranged a job for Vincent as a bookstore clerk. He loved books and worked from eight a.m. until midnight. When the store flooded, he astounded his colleagues with his sheer physical endurance as he carried pile after pile of books to safety. His goal had become to get accepted to a university so that he could later train as a pastor. He worked with a tutor and copied the text of entire books by hand. "I must sit up as long as I can keep my eyes open," he told his brother. He reminded himself that "practice makes perfect," but Latin and Greek did not come easily to him. Vincent resolved he would begin work before his peers woke up and finish after they slept.

But, still, he floundered in his studies and in trying to find his path. At twenty-seven, a full decade after an exciting start as an art dealer, he had no possessions, no accomplishments, nor did he have any sense of direction for what he wanted to do or be.

He poured his heart out in a letter to his little brother, who was now a respected art dealer himself. Vincent compared himself to a caged bird in spring who feels deeply that it is time for him to do something important but cannot recall what it is and so "bangs his head against the bars of his cage." A man, too, he insisted, "doesn't always know himself what he could do, but he feels by instinct, I'm good for something, even so! . . . There's something within me, so what is it!" He had been a student, an art dealer, a teacher, a bookseller, and more. After promising starts, he had failed spectacularly in every path he tried.

His brothers suggested he try carpentry or look for work as a barber. His sister thought he would make a fine baker. He was an insatiable reader, so perhaps a librarian. But, in the depths of his despair, Vincent turned his ferocious energy on the last thing he could think of that he could start right away. His next letter to his brother was very short: "I'm writing to you while drawing and I'm in a hurry to get back to it." Previously, Vincent had believed drawing to be a distraction. Now he began to seek truth by documenting the lives around him in drawings. He started at the very beginning, reading a French book for novices called *The Guide to the ABCs of Drawing*.

His former art-dealer boss pronounced his drawings unworthy of being displayed for sale. "Of one thing I am sure," he told him, "you are no artist." He added flatly, "You started too late." Imagine if Vincent had listened to him.

In the coming years, he would make a few very brief attempts at formal art training. When he was nearly thirty-three, Vincent enrolled in art school alongside students ten years younger than him, but he lasted only a few weeks. He entered the class drawing competition, and the judges harshly suggested he switch into a beginner's class with ten-year-old students.

Just as he had between different careers, Vincent pinballed from one artistic passion to another. On one day, he felt true artists only painted realistic images of people. When his figures came out poorly, the next day he decided that true artists only cared for landscapes. One day he strived for realism, another for abstract expression. One year, he decided all true art consisted only of shades of black and gray, and then later that vibrant color was the real pearl inside the artist's shell. Each time, he fell fully in love, then just as fully and quickly back out.

One day, he dragged an easel and oil paints—with which he had almost no experience—out to a sand dune in a storm. He ran in and out of cover, slapping and slathering paint on the canvas in quick strokes between gusts of wind that peppered the painting with grains of sand. He squeezed color right from the tube onto the canvas when he had to. More than a century later, his definitive biographers would write of that day, "[He] made an astonishing discovery: he could paint." And he felt it. "I enjoy it tremendously," he wrote his brother. "Painting has proved less difficult than I expected."

He continued to leap from one artistic experiment to another. He obsessed over deeper and darker blacks in colorless works, then dispensed with that in favor of vibrant color, his about-face so thorough that he would not even use black to depict the night sky. He started piano lessons because he thought musical tones might teach him something about color tones.

He finally left behind all of the styles that he had previously claimed to be important—but at which he had failed—and he emerged with a new art. It was slathered with paint, erupting with color. He wanted to make art that anyone could understand, not snooty works for those with privileged training. For years he had tried and failed to capture every proportion of a human figure accurately. Now he let that go so entirely that he painted figures walking among trees with faces left blank and hands like mittens.

One evening, he looked out his bedroom window toward the rolling hills in the distance and, as he had with birds and beetles as a boy, watched the sky pass for hours. When he picked up the paintbrush, his imagination transformed a nearby town into a tiny village, its towering church to a humble chapel. The dark-green cypress tree in the foreground became massive, winding up the canvas like seaweed in the swirling rhythm of the night sky.

That painting became one of Van Gogh's most famous, *The Starry Night*. It, along with the many other paintings in Vincent's new style—the style he devised amid a succession of failures—would launch a new era of art and inspire new concepts of beauty and expression. Paintings that he dashed off in hours as experiments over the final two years of his short life would become some of the most valuable objects that have ever existed in the world.

Jackson Pollock

The artist and writer Steven Naifeh told me that the American artist Jackson Pollock, who was best known for creating large paintings by dripping and pouring paint onto his canvases "was literally one of the least talented draftsmen at the Art Students League." He suggested that, like Van Gogh, Pollock's lack of traditional drawing skill was what led him to invent his own rules for making art.

Vincent van Gogh's work now graces everything from socks to cell phone cases. Four of his paintings have sold for more than $100 million (adjusted for inflation), and they weren't even the most famous ones. But Van Gogh's reach stretches far beyond money. "What artists do changed because of Vincent van Gogh," Steven Naifeh told me. Van Gogh's paintings served as a bridge to modern art.

And yet if Van Gogh, who died at just age thirty-seven, had passed away even a few years before he did, would anyone still know his name today?

It would be easy enough to cherry-pick stories like Van Gogh's, stories of exceptional late developers overcoming the odds. But he isn't an exception because of his late starts. And his late starts did not stack the odds against him. In fact, his late start was integral to his eventual success. Van Gogh is just one example of someone who took advantage of a sampling period. He dived into different activities, learning about his own interests and abilities and changing direction based on what he learned until he found high match quality.

"Match quality" is a term that describes the amount of fit between the work or activity someone does and who they are—how their abilities match up with what they like. If someone who loves to ski and enjoys cold weather finds work as a ski instructor, they have high match quality. If you ask a person who strongly dislikes math class and struggles to complete their homework to be your math tutor, you will have a tutor with low match quality.

The economist Ofer Malamud was inspired to study match quality because of his own personal experience. Ofer grew up in Hong Kong and attended an English school that required him to choose a specialization in the last two years of high school. "When you applied to college in England, you had to apply to a specific major," he told me. At first he thought he'd choose engineering because his father was an engineer. But at the last moment he chose not to pick a specialty and applied to colleges in the U.S. instead—"I didn't know what I wanted to do," he said.

Ofer ended up sampling different subjects before he found what was right for him, which turned out to be economics and then philosophy. His own experience left him wondering about how the timing of when someone specializes in a subject impacts their career choice. The question he studied was, Who usually won the trade-off, early or late specializers? He analyzed data from thousands of former students in England, Wales, and Scotland. Students in England and Wales during the period he studied were required to specialize before they started college and to choose specific, narrow programs of study. In Scotland, on the other hand, students were actually required to study various fields during their first two years of college, and they could keep sampling beyond that.

Ofer Malamud found that because they had less sampling opportunity, more English and Welsh students headed down a narrow path before they knew whether it was a good path for them. They were specializing so early that they were making more mistakes when it came to match quality. Malamud concluded that learning stuff was less important than learning about oneself. Exploration and sampling isn't a luxury when it comes to education. It's a central benefit.

Do Quitters Win?

The idea that people who sample among options and change their chosen jobs or sports or activities have an advantage seems to fly in the face of the old concept that quitters never win. But switchers are winners.

Seth Godin is the author of a book that mocks the notion that quitters never win. Instead, Godin argues that "winners" quit fast and often when they feel that a plan is not the best fit. And they don't feel bad about it. "We fail," he writes, when we stick with "tasks we don't have the guts to quit." Godin doesn't suggest quitting simply because something is difficult. Persevering through difficulty is beneficial in the long run. But he does suggest that knowing when to quit yields a big strategic advantage. It's such an advantage that before beginning any undertaking, everyone should take time to think about when and why they would quit. The important trick, Godin says, is staying attuned to whether quitting is really a failure of perseverance or a recognition of low match quality.

I was not close to the worst 800-meter runner on my Division I college track team my freshman year; I was *the* worst, by a landslide. I was allowed to keep practicing with the team because as long as you are not chosen for travel, it doesn't cost anybody anything. I stuck with it for two miserable years of vomit-inducing workouts and ego-bruising races. There were plenty of days (and weeks, and an entire month or three) when I felt like I should probably quit. But I was learning about the kind of training that worked for me, and I was improving. In my senior season, I cracked the university's all-time top-ten list indoors, was twice All-East, and was part of a relay that set the university record. Hilariously, I was awarded the Gustave A. Jaeger Memorial Prize for the athlete who "achieved significant athletic success in the face of unusual challenge and difficulty"—my "unusual challenge and difficulty" just being that I epically stunk at first. After the presentation, the head coach, with whom I'd had little direct conversation, shared that he had felt sorry for me watching workouts my freshman year.

There's nothing particularly special about that story—someone has to start as the worst on every team. But I think it is indicative of my approach to work today. When I was seventeen years old, I was positive that I was going to go to the U.S. Air Force Academy for college to become a pilot and then an astronaut. But I never did any of that.

At the last minute, I changed my mind and decided to study political science in college. Instead, I ended up studying earth and environmental sciences and astronomy, certain I would become a scientist. Then I worked in labs during and after college and realized that I was not the type of person who wanted to spend my entire life learning one or two things new to the world. I wanted to constantly learn things new to me and share them. So I transitioned from science to journalism; my first job was as a midnight-shift street reporter covering crime in New York City.

As my self-knowledge grew, I kept changing my goals and interests until I landed in a career that demands investigating broad interests. When I worked at *Sports Illustrated*, determined students would ask me whether it was better to study journalism or English to get a job at a sports magazine. I told them I had no clue, but that a statistics or biology course never hurt anyone.

Musical Range

Seventeenth-century Venice was not an easy place for a child to be an orphan. One exception may have been a group of girls who had each been left as a baby at the doorstep of an institution known as the Ospedale della Pietà, or "Hospital of Pity." The girls who grew up at the Pietà received an extraordinary education in music. Famed composer Antonio Vivaldi would go on to write 140 concertos exclusively for the Pietà musicians.

The Pietà's music program was not extraordinary because of its rigor. Actually, according to documents, formal lessons only occurred a few times a week, on Tuesdays, Thursdays, and Saturdays, and the girls were free to practice on their own. Work and chores took most of their time instead, and at one point they were only allowed one hour a day of music study. They were not playing or practicing an unusual amount.

Instead, the most surprising feature of their music education was how many instruments they learned. One eyewitness account reported an "excellent concert, performed by female violins, [oboes], tenors, basses, harpsichords, French horns, and even double basses." More surprising still, "these young persons frequently changed instruments." In fact, the Pietà girls learned to play every instrument their institution owned (and also took singing lessons). It helped that they were paid for learning new skills, which would have provided some good motivation.

This multi-instrument background had a practical importance throughout their lives. One Pietà girl who started on the bass and moved to the violin, then to the oboe, was able to return to the violin when her teeth fell out when she was over sixty years old. (Teeth are needed to play the oboe.) After switching back to the violin, she continued performing into her seventies.

These girls weren't merely playing a surprising number of instruments well, they were also participants in an extraordinary period for instrument invention. Some of the instruments they are known to have learned to play are so obscure nobody knows what exactly they were. The Pietà girls lifted composers to new heights and are a part of classical music history. Their skills on a vast array of instruments enabled musical experimentation so important that it laid a foundation for the modern orchestra.

Their stories, though, were largely forgotten or lost. Maybe the memories of them faded because they were women during the seventeenth century. Or maybe because so many of them had no family to speak of. It's easy to imagine how sensational the Pietà girls would be today: *A world-famous orchestra made up of orphans! You will be treated to virtuoso solos on instruments you know and love as well as ones you've never heard of! Occasionally during the show, the musicians will all switch instruments!*

The strategies behind the Pietà girls' musical development would be a hard sell today, though. The multi-instrument approach seems to go against our idea about how to get good at a skill like playing music. It certainly goes against the highly focused deliberate-practice framework

> that's so common. Learning multiple instruments, from that perspective, would be a waste of time. But just as Roger Federer broadened his skills by playing many sports as a kid, in the long run the Pietà girls' work playing multiple instruments helped them expand their range and simply made them better musicians.

There are, of course, outstanding musicians who have focused very young. World-renowned cellist Yo-Yo Ma is a well-known example. Less well known, though, is the fact that Ma started on violin and moved to piano and then to the cello because he didn't really like the first two instruments. He just went through the sampling period a lot faster than a typical music student. Young people often have their goals set for them, whether by parents, teachers, coaches, or other well-meaning adults. And even if specific expectations aren't preset, there is probably

a limit on the options a young person can choose from in the first place. When you're doing an activity that's been preselected for you, pursuing it with passion and resilience is a challenge. But sticking with something for the sake of sticking with it can get in the way of high match quality. And finding high match quality in the first place is the greater challenge.

At every job he had, Van Gogh was convinced that if he outworked everyone around him, he would succeed. But then he would fail anyway. His interests changed constantly. Even once he'd set himself on being an artist, he would devote all his energy to one style or medium only to completely give it up soon thereafter. He was, his biographers wrote, "a paragon of persistence in the face of adversity."

No one in their right mind would argue that passion and perseverance are unimportant or that a bad day is a cue to quit. But the idea that a change of interest is an imperfection and a competitive disadvantage is problematic. It leads to the simple, one-size-fits-all, Tiger Woods story of narrow specialization: pick and stick, as soon as possible, and, above all, do not change the plan. Responding to your lived experience and reaction to something by changing direction, like Van Gogh did so frequently, may be less tidy, but it's no less important. And it improves your chances of finding high match quality. Switchers are often winners.

QUESTIONS

1. Vincent van Gogh discovered his artistic talent late in his life, after years of trying many different careers. How do you think his life might have been different if he had not tried so many different jobs?

2. We've seen that sampling different activities and experiences is an important part of figuring out what you like to do. Quitting might sound bad, but sometimes it's actually the smartest thing you can do. How might you figure out when it's time to change things up?

3. Can you think of an example of high match quality in your own life? Is there an activity you do that feels just right for you? If you don't feel like you have that yet, what are some ways you might search for better match quality?

3

Don't Plan on It

Frances Hesselbein was born in 1915 and grew up in the mountains of western Pennsylvania, among steel mills and coal mines. "In Johnstown, 5:30 means 5:30," she often said. So if the executives, military officers, and politicians who once lined up outside the door of her Manhattan office seeking her advice wanted a full hour to meet with her, they had to be on time. Even after she turned one hundred years old, Frances went to the office every weekday. She was fond of telling visitors that she had held only four professional jobs, and she had never applied for a single one of them. In fact, she attempted to turn down three of the positions. Whenever she tried to guess where life would take her, Frances was pretty much always wrong.

In high school, she dreamed of being a playwright. After graduation, she enrolled in the University of Pittsburgh's Junior College. She loved experimenting with different classes, but her father fell ill during her first year. Frances was just seventeen and the eldest of three siblings when he passed away. She kissed him on the forehead and promised to take care of the family. She finished the semester, then dropped out to work as an assistant at a department store.

She soon got married and had a son just in time for her husband, John Hesselbein, to report to the navy during World War II. John served as a combat aircrew photographer, and when he came home he set up a photography studio, doing everything from high school portraits to documentary films. Frances had the job she called "helping John." If a customer wanted a photo of a dog to look like a painting, she grabbed oil paints and colored it. Anything for a happy customer.

Frances Hesselbein adored her hometown's rich diversity, but, like many places, Johnstown offered up some ugly lessons. As part of the newly formed Pennsylvania Human Relations Commission, John responded to acts of discrimination in town, like a barbershop that would not cut Black customers' hair. "I don't have the right tools," the barber complained. John's response: "Then you will have to buy the right tools." Frances decided that a community that valued inclusiveness should answer "yes" to the question, When they look at us, can they find themselves?

When Frances was thirty-four, a prominent woman in the community stopped by her home and asked her to volunteer to lead Girl Scout Troop 17. The previous leader had left to become a missionary in India, and other neighbors had turned down the request. So did Frances, three times. She had an eight-year-old boy and professed to know nothing about little girls. But when the woman finally said that the group of thirty ten-year-old girls from modest families who met in a church basement would have to be disbanded, Frances agreed to stand in for six weeks until a real leader was found.

In preparation, she read up on the Girl Scouts. She learned that the organization was founded in 1912, eight years before women could vote in the United States, and that the founder had reminded girls that they could be "a doctor, a lawyer, an aviatrix, or a hot-air balloonist." Frances thought back to when she had been in second grade and announced that she wanted to be a pilot. Her classmates had laughed at her. So she showed up in the church basement to start her six weeks as the troop's leader. She ended up staying with Troop 17 for eight years, until they graduated high school.

After that, Frances kept picking up Girl Scouts roles she neither sought nor intended to keep. She was in her mid-forties when she left the United States for the first time, for an international Girl Scouts meeting in Greece. More trips followed—India, Thailand, Kenya. Frances realized she loved volunteering.

In 1970, a trio of Johnstown business leaders who supported the Girl Scouts invited Frances to lunch. They told her that they had chosen a new executive director of the local Girl Scouts council. The previous one had left, and the council was in serious financial trouble.

"How wonderful, who is it?" she asked.

"You," they replied.

"I would never take a professional job," she told them. "I am a volunteer."

They finally talked her into it, sort of. She agreed to fill in for only six months and then to step aside for an experienced professional. This was the beginning of what she called her first professional job. She was fifty-four years old. Frances read management books to prepare and soon realized that the work fit her. She stayed for four years.

But even as her work was going well, the bigger picture wasn't so great. In the late 1960s and early 1970s, society changed dramatically. The Girl Scouts organization did not. Girls were preparing for college and careers in unprecedented numbers, and they needed information on topics like sex and drugs. The organization was in crisis, as membership plummeted and its top leadership position went unfilled for nearly an entire year. In 1976, the committee searching for the next chief executive officer of the Girl Scouts invited Frances Hesselbein to New York City for an interview. Previous Girl Scouts CEOs had staggering leadership credentials. The most recent chief executive was Dr. Cecily Cannan Selby, who started at Radcliffe College at just sixteen years old and later used her physical biology PhD from the Massachusetts Institute of Technology to apply wartime technology to the study of cells. Selby had held a variety of national leadership positions. Hesselbein, meanwhile, had been the head of a local Girl Scouts council, one of 335 around the country. She planned to spend her life in Pennsylvania, so she politely turned down the interview.

But her husband, John, insisted that if she was going to decline the job, he would drive her to New York City so she could do it in person. Since she was not interested in the job, she felt at ease when the committee asked her what she would do if she were to become CEO. Frances described the total transformation of an organization steeped in tradition: activities reworked to stay relevant—heavy on math, science, and technology; the leadership structure dismantled and reimagined so that staff at all levels could advance ideas from local councils toward the national decision-makers at the center. Finally, the organization would be inclusive: when girls of all backgrounds looked at the Girl Scouts, they would have to find themselves.

Which is how Frances found herself accepting a job she'd tried not to interview for. She arrived in New York City on July 4, 1976, as CEO of a three-million-member organization. Out went the standard handbook in favor of four handbooks, each targeted at a specific age group. She hired artists and told them that a six-year-old indigenous girl near an ice floe in Alaska who flipped through a handbook had better see someone who looked like her in a Girl Scouts uniform. She commissioned research on messaging to invite girls of all backgrounds to join the organization. It culminated in poetic marketing posters. One targeted at Native

Americans read, "Your names are on the rivers."

Diversity was great, Frances was told, but it was too much too soon. Fix the organizational problems and then worry about diversity. But Frances had decided that diversity was the Girl Scouts' main problem, so she took it further. She assembled a leadership team that represented her target audience and modernized everything, from the Girl Scouts mission statement to the merit badges. There would now be badges for math and learning about computers. She made the difficult decision to sell campgrounds that volunteers and staff members adored from their youth but that were no longer getting enough use.

Hesselbein remained CEO for thirteen years. Under her leadership, membership of girls from minority groups tripled; the Girl Scouts added a quarter million members and more than 130,000 new volunteers. The famous Girl Scouts Cookies business grew to more than $300 million a year.

In 1990, Frances was in her mid-seventies and retired from the Girl Scouts, though she wasn't done working. In fact, she kept at it until well after her hundredth birthday. (She passed away in 2022 at the remarkable age of 107.) When I first visited just after she turned 101, I brought her a cup of steamed milk, as I had been advised, and right away asked what training had prepared her for leadership. Wrong question. "Oh, don't ask me what my training was," she replied with a dismissing hand wave. She explained that she just did whatever seemed like it would teach her something and allow her to be of service at each moment, and somehow that added up to training. "I was unaware that I was being prepared," she told me. "I did not intend to become a leader; I just learned by doing what was needed at the time."

Frances never did graduate from college, but her office walls were covered with twenty-three honorary doctorates, plus a glistening saber given to her by the U.S. Military Academy for teaching leadership courses, as well as the Presidential Medal of Freedom, the highest civilian award in the United States.

She saw the power of both inclusion and exclusion in her diverse hometown. She learned resourcefulness when she assisted her husband with his photography business. As a new troop leader with less experience than the scouts she was leading, she relied on shared leadership. Having never been out of the country until she traveled to international Girl Scouts meetings, she learned to quickly find common ground with peers from all over the world.

At the first-ever Girl Scouts training event Frances attended, she heard another new troop leader complain that she wasn't learning anything from the session. Frances mentioned it to another volunteer, and the woman told her, "You have to carry a big basket to bring something home." The wisdom stuck with Frances, and she repeated that phrase often. To her, it meant that a mind kept wide open will take something from every new experience.

It was a natural philosophy for someone who was sixty years old when she attempted to turn down an interview for the job that became her calling. She had no long-term plan, only a plan to do what was interesting or needed at the moment. "I never envisioned" were words she spoke often.

Frances Hesselbein's professional career, which didn't start until she was in her mid-fifties, was extraordinary. Her meandering path, however, was not. Instead of worrying about a long-term plan, she responded to interesting opportunities to do meaningful work that were right in front of her. Research has shown that people who focus on finding a good fit rather than worrying about a specific career path are more successful. "They focused on, 'Here's who I am at the moment, here are my motivations, here's what I've found I like to do, here's what I'd like to learn, and here are the opportunities. Which of these is the best match right now? And maybe a year from now I'll switch because I'll find something better,'" the neuroscientist Ogi Ogas, who has coauthored research on how people find good career matches, said to me. They have an unusual journey but a common strategy. "Short-term planning," Ogas told me. "They all practice it, not long-term planning."

Drop Your Tools

Psychologist Karl Weick noticed something unusual when he studied wildland firefighters. When he looked at firefighters who died in the line of duty fighting wildfires, he found they held on to their tools. Even when ditching their equipment would have allowed them to run away from an advancing fire, they kept it with them.

Weick had seen similar reactions in navy seamen who ignored orders to remove their steel-toed shoes when abandoning a ship. Some of them had gone on to drown or punch holes in their life rafts with their boots. He'd also studied fighter pilots who refused to eject from disabled planes. "It is the very unwillingness of people to drop their tools that turns some of these dramas into tragedies," he wrote. Weick found that dropping one's tool represented a sort of unlearning, or willingness to adapt or be flexible.

With his work, Weick saw that rather than adapting to unfamiliar situations, experienced groups could become rigid under pressure. And when that inflexibility happens, it leads them to "regress to what they know best." They attempt to bend an unfamiliar situation to a familiar comfort zone, as if trying to will it into something they have actually experienced before.

For wildland firefighters, their tools are what they know best. "Firefighting tools define the firefighter's group membership, they are the firefighter's reason for being deployed in the first place," Weick wrote. "Given the central role of tools in defining the essence of a firefighter, it is not surprising that dropping one's tools creates" a kind of mental crisis. As Norman Maclean, the author of a book about a 1949 firefighter tragedy, put it, "When a firefighter is told to drop his firefighting tools, he is told to forget he is a firefighter."

Weick explained that wildland firefighters have a "can do" culture and that dropping their tools is not a part of that culture because it would mean they had lost control of a situation. There are certain times where a "can do" attitude should be swapped for what he calls a "make do" culture, though. There are times when it's important to improvise and to resist being trapped by familiar or established procedures.

It is easy to say *they should have done this, not that* about another group of people, or when looking back to study moments in history. It's easy to think it about someone you know, a friend or a teammate, for example, who—to you—clearly made a poor choice. But it's very difficult to think that way about yourself in the midst of a stressful or new situation. We all have a tendency to cling to the familiar, especially in the face of an unfamiliar scenario. So it's valuable to understand there is no tool that cannot be dropped, reimagined, or repurposed in order to navigate a new challenge.

People who embrace the idea of range live by the historian Arnold Toynbee's words that no tool works in all situations: "There is no such thing as a master-key that will unlock *all* doors." Rather than possessing a single tool, people with range collect an entire toolshed and show the power of range in a hyper-specialized world.

Even people who look like long-term visionaries from afar usually look like short-term planners up close. When Nike cofounder Phil Knight was asked in 2016 about his long-term vision and how he knew what he wanted when he created the company, he replied that he had actually known he wanted to be a professional athlete. But he was not good enough, so he shifted to simply trying to find some way to stay involved with sports. He happened to run track under a college coach who tinkered with shoes and who later became his cofounder.

"I feel sorry for the people who know exactly what they're going to do from the time they're sophomores in high school," he said. In his memoir, Knight wrote that he "wasn't much for setting goals" and that his main goal for his shoe company was to fail fast enough that he could apply what he was learning to his next venture. He made one short-term pivot after another, applying the lessons as he went.

The author and screenwriter of *Jurassic Park*, Michael Crichton, started in medicine, after learning how few writers earn enough money to make a living. With medicine, "I would never have to wonder if the work was worthwhile," he wrote. Except a few years in he became disenchanted with medical practice. He graduated from Harvard Medical School but decided to become a writer. His medical education was not remotely wasted. He used it to craft some of the most popular stories in the world.

When she was young, award-winning mathematician Maryam Mirzakhani actually expected to be a novelist. She was enchanted by bookstores near her school and dreamed of writing. She had to take math classes, but "I was just not interested in thinking about it," she said later. Eventually she came to see math as exploration. "It is  like being lost in a jungle and trying to use all the knowledge that you can gather to come up with some new tricks, and with some luck, you might find a way out." In 2014, she became the first woman to win the Fields Medal, the most famous math prize in the world.

Fantasy author Patrick Rothfuss began studying chemical engineering in college, which "led to a revelation that chemical engineering is boring." He then spent *nine years* bouncing between majors "before being kindly asked to graduate already." Meanwhile, he was slowly working on a novel. That novel, *The Name of the Wind*, sold millions of copies worldwide. The book also happens to feature a lot of chemistry.

Hillary Jordan, who just happened to be my downstairs neighbor in a Brooklyn apartment building, told me that she worked in advertising for fifteen years before beginning to write fiction. Her first novel, *Mudbound*, was a prize winner that was later adapted into a feature film, starring Mary J. Blige, which received four Oscar nominations.

Of the athletes I met when I worked at *Sports Illustrated*, the one I most admired was British Ironman triathlete (and writer and humanitarian) Chrissie Wellington, who got on a road bike for the first time in her life at age twenty-seven. She was working on a sewage sanitation project in Nepal when she found that she enjoyed cycling and could keep up with the native Sherpas at high altitudes in the Himalayas. Two years after returning home, she won the first of four Ironman World Championships and then proceeded to go 13–0 at the Ironman distance over the course of a career that started late and lasted just five years. When she retired, Wellington said, "My passion for the sport hasn't waned, but my passion for new experiences and new challenges is what is now burning most brightly."

"Outsider Art"

There has been an explosion of interest in a kind of art that's often called "outsider art," which refers to art created by artists who are self-taught or who have not received formal training. They begin their careers outside of the standard path of traditional art school. Of course, there is nothing wrong with coming through a formal talent-development system such as art school, but if that's the only pipeline that exists, some of the brightest talents get missed. "Outsider artists" are self-taught masters of visual art, and the originality of their work can be stunning.

Katherine Jentleson, who in 2015 was appointed as a full-time curator of self-taught art at the High Museum of Art in Atlanta, told me that these artists typically started just by experimenting and doing things they liked while working other jobs. "The majority did not begin their art making in earnest until after retirement," Jentleson said.

She introduced me to the sculptor and painter Lonnie Holley, a prominent self-taught artist who grew up extremely poor in Alabama. In 1979, when he was twenty-nine, his sister's two children died in a fire. The family could not afford grave-stones, so Holley gathered discarded sandstone at a nearby foundry and carved them himself. "I didn't even know what art was!" he told me, his eyes wide, as if taken by surprise at his own story. But it felt good. He carved gravestones for other families and started making sculptures out of any-thing he could find. I was standing with him near the door of an Atlanta gallery featuring his work when he grabbed a paper clip and quickly bent it into an intricate silhouette of a face, which he jabbed decoratively into the eraser of a pencil the woman at the front desk was using. It is hard to imagine a time before he made art, since it seems like he can hardly touch something before his hands begin exploring what else it might become.

Jentleson also pointed me to Paradise Garden, the painting- and sculpture-filled property of the late minister Howard Finster, ninety miles northwest of Atlanta. Finster had long compiled displays on his land, from collections of tools to assortments of fruit-bearing plants. He was fixing a bicycle one day in 1976, when he was fifty-nine, and saw what looked like a face in a splotch of white paint on his thumb. "A warm feelin' come over my body," he recalled. Finster immediately began creating what became tens of thousands of artworks that filled his property, including thousands of paintings in his unique, semi-cartoonish style, often densely packed with animals and figures. Soon enough, he was appearing on TV and creating album covers for bands such as R.E.M. and Talking Heads. Upon entry to the garden, I was greeted by a giant self-portrait of a smirking Finster in a burgundy suit, affixed to a cinderblock wall. At the bottom are the words "I began painting pictures in Jan-1976—without any training. This is my painting. A person don't know what he can do unless he tryes. Trying things is the answer to find your talent."

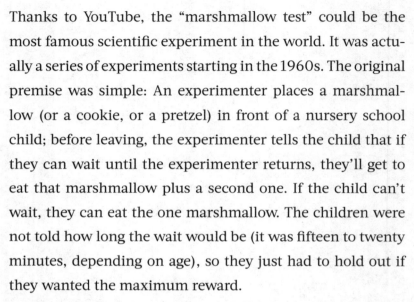

Thanks to YouTube, the "marshmallow test" could be the most famous scientific experiment in the world. It was actually a series of experiments starting in the 1960s. The original premise was simple: An experimenter places a marshmallow (or a cookie, or a pretzel) in front of a nursery school child; before leaving, the experimenter tells the child that if they can wait until the experimenter returns, they'll get to eat that marshmallow plus a second one. If the child can't wait, they can eat the one marshmallow. The children were not told how long the wait would be (it was fifteen to twenty minutes, depending on age), so they just had to hold out if they wanted the maximum reward.

Psychologist Walter Mischel and his research team followed up with the children who participated in the experiment years later and found that the longer a child had been able to wait during the marshmallow test, the more likely they were to be successful socially, academically, and financially, and the less likely they were to abuse drugs.

Mischel's collaborator Yuichi Shoda has repeatedly made a point of saying that plenty of preschoolers who couldn't wait and ate the marshmallow were just fine later in life. Shoda maintains that the most exciting aspect of the studies was demonstrating how easily children could learn to change a specific behavior with simple mental strategies, like thinking about the marshmallow as a cloud rather than food.

Just like behavior can change, it turns out that people's personalities change more than we might expect during their lives. Time, life experiences, and the different situations we face all influence the kind of people we are. And because who we are changes as we get older, it's hard to set long-term goals when we're young. People who are younger usually haven't had enough time or life experiences to figure out their likes and dislikes yet. Each "story of me" continues to evolve. We should all heed the wisdom of Alice in Lewis Carroll's *Alice's Adventures in Wonderland*—when asked by the Gryphon to share her story, Alice decided she had to start with the beginning of her adventure that very morning. "It's no use going back to yesterday," she said, "because I was a different person then."

Who we each are is a combination of numerous possibilities. As Herminia Ibarra, a business school professor, explained it to me, "We discover the possibilities by *doing*, by trying new activities, building new networks, finding new role models." We learn who we are in practice, not in theory. Think of Frances Hesselbein, who assumed over and over that she was just dipping her toe into something new temporarily. It took until she was well over fifty years old for her to finally realize she had short-term-planned her way to an extraordinary career. Or remember Vincent van Gogh, who was certain he found the perfect job again and again, only to learn in practice that he was mistaken, until he wasn't.

Paul Graham is a computer scientist and cofounder of Y Combinator, which funded start-up companies including Airbnb and Twitch. He touched on ideas that are similar to Ibarra's in a talk he wrote for a high school:

It might seem that nothing would be easier than deciding what you like, but it turns out to be hard, partly because it's hard to get an accurate picture of most jobs . . . Most of the work I've done in the last ten years didn't exist when I was in high school . . . In such a world it's not a good idea to have fixed plans.

And yet every May, speakers all over the country fire up the Standard Graduation Speech, the theme of which is: don't give up on your dreams. I know what they mean, but this implies you're supposed to be bound by some plan you made early on . . .

In the graduation-speech approach, you decide where you want to be in twenty years, and then ask: What should I do now to get there? I propose instead that you don't commit to anything in the future, but just look at the options available now, and choose those that will give you the most promising range of options afterward.

Popular lore holds that the sculptor Michelangelo would see a full figure in a solid block of marble before he ever touched it and then simply chip away the excess stone to free the figure he'd envisioned inside. It is an exquisitely beautiful idea. It just isn't true. The art historian William Wallace showed that Michelangelo was actually a test-and-learn all-star. He constantly changed his mind and altered his sculptural plans as he worked. He left three-fifths of his sculptures unfinished, each time moving on to something more promising. He tried, then went from there. He was a sculptor, painter, and master architect, and he made engineering designs for fortifications in Florence, Italy. In his late twenties he even pushed visual art aside to spend time writing poems (including one about how much he grew to dislike painting), half of which he left unfinished.

Michelangelo learned who he was—and whom he was carving—in practice, not in theory. He learned by doing. He started with an idea, tested it, changed it, and readily abandoned it for a better project fit. He worked according to Ibarra's idea: "I know who I am when I see what I do."

The same was true for Titus Kaphar. Nobody in his family went to college, as he tells it. His mother didn't go to college. His father went to prison, but not to college. Neither his grandmother nor his grandfather went to college. Nobody went to college. Except—he corrects himself—a distant cousin. Titus himself certainly wasn't going to college. He often didn't go to high school.

And yet, in his twenties, he decided to enroll in a few junior college classes. As he explained to me, he wanted to date a soon-to-be teacher, and she was not impressed that he had no plans for the future.

"So I just went over to the junior college," Titus told me, "kind of as a joke, not really taking it seriously, because, you know, I'm not an academic. I'm not a person who does really well in school." He picked a few classes more or less at random. He came back and told the woman he wanted to date. They had a quick laugh about it.

One class he chose was art history. Why? "I probably read

the word 'art' and thought, 'Art should be easy,'" Titus told me. In an unexpected way, it was. Titus realized that he could remember details of paintings—not just remember what he had seen but associate a painting with the style of a particular artist. "I remember one day we were talking about Van Gogh," he recalled, "and I remember seeing the image and being very aware of where the painting sat in the history of art." He began to contribute to class discussions. His confidence grew, and he got a B in the class.

"That was a new experience for me," he said, "a B overall in the class at something that was academic. It made me go, 'Hold up, wait a minute.' I realized this was, in fact, something that I was enjoying, and I could feel myself wanting to push harder." He took more classes and tested strategies until he found something that worked. Suddenly, college didn't seem like such a crazy idea.

Titus enrolled at San Jose State University to study fine arts. Eventually, he took an actual painting class. He began to study paintings and then try to reverse engineer them—recreating what he observed. "That right there is how I learned to paint, by looking a lot." He spent hours in the studio. He got so much better that a professor told him he should apply to graduate school at Yale University.

The next year, he applied to Yale and a bunch of other

graduate schools. He got rejected from all of them. But he'd found his work identity. "I'm an artist," he said. "I'm a maker, so I'm going to make." And that's what he did. His body of work eventually got him into Yale, where he was one of the oldest students in his class.

Today, Titus lives in New Haven, Connecticut, with his family. He and a colleague founded an art space where early-career artists can apply for studio space. Those artists in turn mentor local high school students who are paid to serve as studio assistants. For most of the students, it is their first job of any kind. Titus is now a filmmaker, and in 2018 he received a MacArthur Foundation Fellowship, often known as a "genius grant." He doesn't really like the word "genius," though. It makes it seem as if someone were plopped on Earth magically knowing what to do and how to do it. It doesn't seem like it could apply to someone who accidentally found his path. But in that first junior college class he took just hoping to get a date, Titus told me, "I realized that I had a visual intelligence that no one had ever asked me to use."

QUESTIONS

1. Researchers have found that instead of asking broad and abstract questions when you're imagining your future, such as *Who do I want to be?*, it is better to be a scientist of yourself. Try asking smaller questions that can actually be tested. For example, *Which possibility should I start to explore now?* Or what are some other smaller questions you could quickly answer that might help you learn more about what you like?

2. What's something that you're curious about but that you don't know much about? It could be anything—a certain job, a new technology, a volunteering opportunity, or another part of the world. In a notebook, write down something you can try in order to learn more about that interest. If you keep doing it, this can become your own personal book of small experiments.

3. Think back to when Frances Hesselbein told me, "I did not intend to become a leader; I just learned by doing what was needed at the time." Can you think of a situation where you've learned to do something that was unexpected or that you hadn't planned on? How might it help you in the future?

4. In order to work on "what was needed at the time," Frances kept her eyes open for challenges in her local community. What's a current challenge in your local community? Is there any way you could help work on it?

QUESTIONS

5. Imagine you were a participant in the marshmallow experiment when you were younger. Do you think you would have been able to wait to eat the marshmallow? Or would you have been unable to resist and gobbled up the one marshmallow quickly? How do you think you might react in a similar experiment today?

PART 2

Learning:
It's Supposed to
Be Hard

4

The Struggle Is Real

You probably wouldn't be surprised to learn that classrooms around the world are very different from each other. One study aiming to understand effective math teaching filmed hundreds of class periods from fourth- and eighth-grade classrooms in the United States, Asia, and Europe. The study found that in the Netherlands, students regularly trickled into class late and spent a lot of class time working on their own. (That probably doesn't sound familiar!) In Hong Kong, though, class looked pretty similar to how it does in the United States: teachers' lectures rather than individual work filled most of the time. Some classes kept kids in their seats; others had them approach the board. Some teachers were very energetic; others were serious. The list of differences between classrooms was long, but none of those was associated with differences in student achievement across countries.

There were similarities too. In every classroom in every country, teachers relied on two main types of questions. The more common were a type that can be called "using procedures" questions—basically, asking students to practice something that they'd just learned, which might be anything from multiplying fractions to solving algebraic formulas. Students were asked to use over and over the procedure that had just been taught. Worksheets were often involved.

The other common type of question was a "making connections" question, which connected students to a broader concept rather than just a procedure and practice. Making-connections questions tend to focus on the why instead of just the how. For example, when a teacher asks students not just to solve problems using a certain mathematical strategy but to explain why the strategy works, that's a making-connections question. Or if a teacher asks their students to try to figure out whether a mathematical strategy can be applied in every type of problem, that's another type of making-connections question.

Here are two examples of making-connections questions that may seem familiar to you:

1. "We know the formula for the area of a rectangle is length times width. How can we use the knowledge to find the formula for the area of a triangle?" (This helps prompt a student to connect the concept of a rectangle's area to that of a triangle by seeing that it is half of the rectangle.)

2. "How are fractions related to decimals? Can you convert ¾ to a decimal and explain your process?"

Using-procedures questions and making-connections questions are both useful when it comes to learning, and both types were posed by teachers in every classroom in every country studied.

But an important difference emerged in what teachers did *after* they asked a broader, making-connections question. Rather than letting students struggle with some confusion, teachers often responded to their own questions by giving hints. And those hints changed the kind of question the teacher had asked by turning a making-connections question into a using-procedures question. In changing the type of question that was asked, teachers also changed the kind of learning the students were doing. The teachers' hints allowed the students to turn a more conceptual math problem they didn't understand into a using-procedures one they could more easily solve. As Lindsey Richland, a professor who studies learning, told me, "We're very good, humans are, at trying to do the least amount of work that we have to in order to accomplish a task." When students asked for hints, they were being both clever and efficient. Of course they wanted help to answer the teacher's question—who wouldn't? The problem is that when it comes to learning some concepts, that kind of efficiency can backfire. Hints often end up making the problem too easy. A student gets to the answer more quickly, but they no longer have to make connections between math concepts, so they aren't really learning.

In the United States, about one-fifth of questions given to students began as making-connections problems. But by the time the students were done seeking hints from the teacher and solving the problems, a grand total of zero percent remained making-connections problems. They'd all become using-procedures problems instead. The making-connections problems did not survive the teacher-student interactions. Straightforward, procedure practice—such as correctly completing those worksheets—is important in math, just like it is in golf or chess. But when worksheets are the only way a student is taught and making-connections questions aren't also solved, it's a problem.

Even when students bring home math work that forces them to make connections, Richland told me, "parents are like, 'Lemme show you; there's a faster, easier way.'" So even if the teacher has given making-connections problems for homework, well-meaning parents can end up turning them into using-procedures questions anyway. Adults often aren't comfortable with bewildered kids. They want students' understanding to come quickly and easily. But for learning that is both durable (it sticks) and flexible (it can be applied broadly), *fast and easy* is precisely the problem. Because when students struggle to come up with an answer, that struggle actually enhances the learning that they're doing.

Teachers in every country sometimes fell into the hint-giving trap and changed making-connections questions into using-procedures questions. But in the higher-performing countries plenty of making-connections problems remained unchanged because teachers in those countries managed to avoid giving hints or help. These teachers allowed their classes to struggle to figure out the questions and concepts on their own. In Japan, a little more than half of all problems were making-connections problems, and half of those stayed that way through the solving. An entire class period could be taken up by just one multipart problem as students struggled to learn how to solve it. The process may not be fast or efficient, but it allows for effective and long-lasting learning.

"Some people argue that part of the reason U.S. students don't do as well on international measures of high school knowledge is that they're doing too well in class," Nate Kornell, a cognitive psychologist, told me. U.S. students aren't exposed to as much struggle in the classroom as other, higher-performing countries' students, so the quality of their learning may not be as strong. "What you want is to make it easy to make it hard," he said.

What did he mean by that? Kornell was explaining a concept known as "desirable difficulties," which says that even though an obstacle makes learning more challenging, slower, and more frustrating in the short term, it actually results in better learning in the long term. Excessive hint giving is the opposite of a desirable difficulty. It boosts immediate performance, so students get the answers right, which can look good in the short term. But those hints undermine students' progress in the long run, since the students often may not understand *how* they're getting to their answers.

One example of a desirable difficulty is the "generation effect." It turns out that struggling to come up with—or to generate—an answer on your own enhances the learning process, even if you come up with the wrong answer. The struggle itself is desirable. So remember that even if it feels terrible to get everything wrong when you're studying new material, it's actually part of a larger positive process for your brain. Struggling now will help you retain information later. It's a desirable difficulty. Take this example: Kornell and the psychologist Janet Metcalfe tested sixth graders in the South Bronx on vocabulary learning in order to explore the generation effect. Some of the students received some of the vocabulary words and their definitions together to study. For example, *To discuss something in order to come to an agreement: Negotiate*. For other words, the students were shown only the definition, not the word being defined. Then they were given time to think of the right word, even if they had no clue what it was. Then the correct word was revealed. When the students were tested later, they did way better on the words that had been given definition-first.

Being forced to generate answers is a desirable difficulty that improves later learning even if you come up with the wrong answer. It can even help to be wildly wrong. Psychologists have repeatedly found that the more confident a learner is of their wrong answer, the better the information sticks when they do learn the right answer. Tolerating big mistakes can create the best learning opportunities. And struggling to retrieve information primes the brain for later learning. That's why testing or quizzing yourself can be an effective study tool. Self-testing is a very desirable difficulty because it helps improve learning. Allowing yourself to struggle to learn material is really useful (as long as the right answer is provided eventually).

In your classroom, one topic is probably taught one week and another the next. That's a typical teaching approach, and it's precisely the opposite of what science recommends for creating long-lasting, durable learning. You may be used to each particular concept or skill getting a short period of intense focus, and then the class is on to the next thing, never to return. That approach may seem to make sense, but it avoids another important desirable difficulty when it comes to high-quality learning: "spacing," or distributed practice, which is what it sounds like—leaving time between practice sessions for the same material. You could even call it deliberate not-practicing between rounds of deliberate practice. "There's a limit to how long you should wait," Kornell told me, "but it's longer than people think. It could be anything—studying foreign language vocabulary or learning how to fly a plane—the harder it is, the more you learn." Space between practice sessions enhances learning.

One study separated Spanish vocabulary learners into two groups: one group learned the vocabulary words and was tested on them the same day, and the second group learned the vocabulary words but was tested on them a month later. A full eight years after that, with no studying of the vocabulary in the meantime, the second group remembered 250 percent more of the words. Spacing had made the second group's learning more productive. (The good news is this is just one example. It doesn't take nearly that long to see the positive impact spacing can have on learning.)

When you're studying, try to remember that struggling can be a good thing. It's difficult to accept, but the best learning happens slowly, and doing poorly at first is essential for doing well later. It isn't bad to get an answer right when you're studying. But your progress shouldn't happen too quickly.

And things shouldn't feel too easy. Think about the desirable difficulties that we've covered, like the generation effect and spacing, and recall why they are good for learning. If you're doing too well when you quiz yourself on the material, one simple option is to wait longer before you try again. If your studying and learning feels inefficient because you're struggling to get the correct answers, remember that, in the long run, that's a positive. Frustration during learning is a good sign—a desirable difficulty.

Overall, there is some great news about school in the United States: students today have mastery of basic skills that is superior to students of previous generations. But there's also a challenge: the goals of education have gotten higher. Education professor Greg Duncan found that focusing on using-procedures problems in the classroom worked well forty years ago. But, "increasingly, jobs that pay well require employees to be able to solve unexpected problems," he wrote. Those shifts in the working world demanded changes in schools and education. The truth is that the strategies that current teachers learned back when they were students are no longer good enough for them to use with their own students.

For example, here is a math question from the early-1980s basic-skills test of all public school sixth graders in Massachusetts:

Carol can ride her bike 10 miles per hour. If Carol rides her bike to the store, how long will it take?

To solve this problem, you would need to know:

A. How far it is to the store.

B. What kind of bike Carol has.

C. What time Carol will leave.

D. How much Carol has to spend.

It's pretty straightforward, right? To solve it, a simple mathematical formula (distance = rate × time) can be memorized and applied. Since you already know the rate at which Carol can ride (10 miles per hour), if you also know the distance to the store you can easily figure out how long the trip will take.

Now, here is a question Massachusetts sixth graders got several decades later, in 2011:

Paige, Rosie, and Cheryl each spent exactly $9.00 at the same snack bar.

Paige bought 3 bags of peanuts.

Rosie bought 2 bags of peanuts and 2 pretzels.

Cheryl bought 1 bag of peanuts, 1 pretzel, and 1 milkshake.

1. What is the cost, in dollars, of 1 bag of peanuts? Show or explain how you got your answer.

2. What is the cost, in dollars, of 1 pretzel? Show or explain how you got your answer.

3. What is the total number of pretzels that can be bought for the cost of 1 milkshake? Show or explain how you got your answer.

The 2011 problem requires a student to connect multiple math concepts that then need to be applied to a new situation. A student who hasn't struggled with making-connections questions or who has learned only by filling out worksheets isn't likely to be able to successfully solve the whole problem. Knowledge increasingly needs to be both durable and flexible so that it's long-lasting and capable of being applied broadly.

Modern Thinking

In 1931, a brilliant Russian psychologist named Alexander Luria wanted to study the impact that a rapidly changing country and modernizing world might be having on its people. He wondered whether all the changes might also be changing people's minds. Luria recognized that there were still some remote villages in his country that had not yet been touched by the warp-speed changes of industrial development that the Soviet Union government was forcing on its citizens at the time.

When Luria arrived at the most remote villages, he learned the local language so that he and the other psychologists he brought with him could engage the villagers in relaxed situations. They aimed to understand the villagers' habits of thinking and asked questions or presented tasks designed to help them do that.

Some were very simple: present bundles of wool or silk in an array of colors and ask participants to describe them. Farmers who had experienced some contact with distant cities and who had been exposed to some industrialization easily picked out blue, red, and yellow, sometimes with variations like dark blue or light yellow. The most remote villagers, who were still "premodern," gave more varied color descriptions: cotton in bloom, decayed teeth, a lot of water, sky, pistachio. Then they were asked to sort the yarn into groups. The farmers and young people with even a little formal education did so easily. Even when they did not know the name of a particular color, they had little trouble putting together darker and lighter shades of the same one. The remote villagers, though, refused to even sort the yarn. "It can't be done," they said. Or, "None of them are the same; you can't put them together."

Sorting geometric shapes went similarly. The more contact with modernity a person had had, the more likely they were to understand the abstract concept of "shapes" and to make groups of triangles, rectangles, and circles even if they did not know the shapes' names. The remote villagers, meanwhile, saw nothing alike in a square drawn with solid lines and the same exact square drawn with dotted lines. To a twenty-six-year-old remote villager named Alieva, the solid-line square was obviously a map, and the dotted-line square was a watch. "How can a map and a watch be put together?" she asked incredulously. And Khamid, another remote villager, insisted that filled and unfilled circles could not go together because one was a coin and the other a moon.

The pattern continued for every type of question. When presented with questions that required them to make abstract, or conceptual, groupings, remote villagers relied on practical ideas based on their direct experience. When psychologists

attempted to explain a "which one does not belong" grouping exercise to Rakmat, they gave him
the example of three adults and one child—the
child being obviously different from the others.
Except Rakmat could not see it that way. "The boy
must stay with the others!" he argued. The adults
are working, "and if they have to keep running out
to fetch things, they'll never get the job done, but
the boy can do the running for them." Okay, then,
how about a hammer, a saw, a hatchet, and a log?
Three of them are tools. They are not a group,
Rakmat replied, because they are useless without
the log, so why would they be together?

What about a grouping of a bird, a rifle, a
dagger, and a bullet? You can't possibly remove
one and have a group, a remote villager insisted.
The bullet must be loaded in the rifle to kill the
bird, and "then you have to cut the bird up with
the dagger, since there's no other way to do it."
No amount of explanation or examples could
get remote villagers to use reasoning based on
any concept that was not a concrete part of their
daily lives.

The farmers and students who had begun to

join the modern world were able to practice a kind of thinking that helped them work out guiding principles when given facts or materials, even if they didn't receive instructions, and even when they had never seen the material before.

Some of the changes brought about by modernity seem almost magical. Luria found that most remote villagers did not experience optical illusions the same way as citizens of the industrialized world did. For example, here is what's known as the Ebbinghaus illusion: Which middle circle below looks bigger?

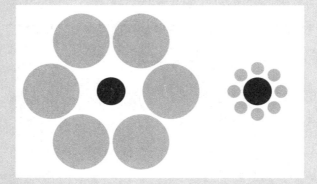

If you said the circle on the right, you're probably a citizen of the modern, industrialized world. The remote villagers saw, correctly, that the middle circles are the same size. Those findings have been repeated elsewhere, and scientists have suggested it may be because premodern people are not as drawn to how the various circles relate to one another, so their perception of the middle circle is not changed by the presence of extra circles. Luria's work helped show that the more someone had been exposed to modernity, the more powerful their abstract thinking was and the less they relied on their concrete, personal experience of the world.

Block It Out

Toward the end of a video recording of an eighth-grade math class that I watched with Professor Lindsey Richland, the students settled into completing a worksheet for what's often called "blocked" practice. This is the most common form of math learning, and it involves practicing the same type of problem over and over.

Imagine your teacher gives you a worksheet

with twenty problems, and all of them are the same kind. For example:

1. ? + 5 = 12
2. ? − 3 = 7
3. ? + 8 = 15

Since every problem follows the same format, you know exactly what to do each time: subtract or add a number to both sides to find the answer You get into a rhythm and solve them quickly because you're using the same method over and over. You don't even have to think about which method to use. Practicing the same thing repeatedly using the same procedure leads to excellent immediate performance. But it doesn't result in flexible learning.

Another psychologist, Doug Rohrer, found that "with blocked practice, students know the strategy for each problem before they read the problem." They know the kind of problems they're working on in a specific block, which can make it look like they understand a concept even if they really don't. Blocking can seem like an efficient form of learning, and it might lead both students and teachers to think effective learning is happening.

Instead of blocking, in order to create learning and knowledge that is flexible, study should happen under varied conditions, an approach called varied or mixed practice. Varied practice improves reasoning skills and allows you to apply what you've learned to other areas. In one study, students who learned math problems in blocks performed a lot worse come test time than students who studied the exact same problems but all mixed up. The blocked-practice students learned procedures for each type of problem through repetition. But the varied-practice students learned how to differentiate types of problems.

Imagine your teacher hands out a worksheet with a mix of different types of problems. The comfort and confidence of all that blocked practice suddenly disappears. A varied-practice worksheet might confuse you because you're not used to identifying different types of problems on your own.

To get a little more specific, here are a few

examples of varied practice:

1. $7 \times 5 = ?$
2. $\frac{7}{8} \times \frac{2}{5} = ?$
3. $42 \div 6 = ?$
4. $\frac{1}{2} + \frac{1}{3} = ?$
5. $9 \times 7 = ?$

With blocked practice, you might feel confident because you're getting the answers right quickly. But when a test comes with new problems of all different types, you might get confused because you're not used to identifying different types of problems on your own.

With varied practice, even though the series of questions is more challenging and might take longer, you're training your brain to recognize different kinds of problems. This makes you better prepared for tests where problems are not sorted by type, and it improves your overall problem-solving skills.

Varied practice is another example of a desirable difficulty. It makes learning harder and slower, but it results in better learning overall.

And varied practice can be applied to both mental and physical skills, whether it's learning a math concept or practicing a new technique during a piano lesson. Varied practice improves a person's ability to match the right strategy to a problem because it strengthens their reasoning skills. And the ability to find the right strategy just happens to be a key feature of expert problem-solving.

The most successful problem solvers spend mental energy figuring out what type of problem they are facing *before* matching a strategy to it rather than jumping in with memorized procedures. Whether they are a chemist working on an experiment or a student facing a tough question on a test, using knowledge that they struggled to learn—and which, therefore, they learned better—will help them solve the problem they're working on.

As we've seen, desirable difficulties like self-testing and spacing make learning more difficult in the short term, but they also make that knowledge stick in the long run. When you struggle, what you learn becomes more durable.

Desirable difficulties slow down learning and can seem inefficient. That can be a problem because everyone wants to be able to see proof of their progress *right now*. But for deeper learning that will be more useful over time (because you'll remember it and because you'll understand it better), it's necessary to learn slowly.

QUESTIONS

1. Why do you think it's difficult for adults such as teachers or parents to resist giving hints to students who are struggling?

2. If you have to learn new material for a test, are you better off studying it all at once right before the test or starting earlier and breaking your studying into several short sessions?

3. The next time you have to prepare for a test, what are some changes you might make to be sure you learn the material as deeply as you can and study as effectively as possible? Do you think you could try self-testing, spacing, or mixed practice?

QUESTIONS

4. Imagine you woke up and went to math class tomorrow in a high-performing classroom in Japan, and the teacher presented only one math problem to solve for the entire class period. Would you feel comfortable with that approach to learning? Do you think you would miss the worksheets and using-procedures questions you may be more familiar with?

5. Remember the generation effect, which says struggling to come up with an answer—even a wrong answer—will prime your brain for better learning when you do see the right answer. It might feel hard to come up with answers for material you don't know well, but that's the point! What's an area of schoolwork where you can quiz yourself in this way even before you know the material well?

5

How to Think Like a Problem Solver

B ack when the seventeenth century was approaching, it was generally accepted that the Earth stayed still while the rest of the universe—the sun, moon, and all observable planets around us—revolved around it. Although astronomer Nicolaus Copernicus had (correctly) proposed that planets moved around the sun, the idea was considered so far-fetched and frightening at the time that people were punished for teaching it.

Like most people, German astronomer Johannes Kepler had also accepted that the Earth didn't move. At first. But then the constellation Cassiopeia suddenly gained a new star. (It was actually an exploding star that made a new light in the sky.) That change led Kepler to recognize that the idea of unmoving planets could not be correct.

By 1596, when he turned twenty-five, Kepler had accepted Copernicus's model of planets orbiting the sun. And now he posed another big question: Why do planets that are farther away from the sun move more slowly? Did these more distant planets have weaker "moving souls"? But why would that be? Just coincidence? Was there a soul or spirit inside the sun, which for some reason acted more powerfully on nearby planets? No one had ever publicly pursued questions like these before. Kepler was so far outside the bounds of previous ideas and thought that there was no existing evidence for him to work from. So, to try to explain how the universe worked, he turned to analogies. He would compare unrelated ideas he knew about to try to help himself answer his own questions.

For example, Kepler knew that smells and heat fade predictably the farther they get away from their source. So he considered whether a mysterious planet-moving power from the sun might work the same way. But he dismissed that idea and moved on to thinking about light.

Light "makes its nest in the sun," Kepler wrote, and yet light appears not to exist between its source and the object it lights up. If light could exist without being visible, so could some other physical entity. He began using words we think of as more scientific, such as "power" or "force," instead of more mystical-sounding terms like "soul" and "spirit." The "moving power" Kepler was thinking about inside the sun was really a precursor to understanding the existence of gravity. The fact that he was thinking about it at all is astounding because he had these thoughts before science had embraced the idea of physical forces that act throughout the universe. This was the sixteenth century, after all, and spirits were still believed to be responsible for moving the planets around. Kepler was working with no evidence and no way to prove his ideas.

When Kepler read a newly published description of magnetism, he thought maybe the planets were like magnets, with poles at either end. He had realized that each planet moved more slowly when it was farther in its orbit from the sun, so maybe the planets and the sun were attracting and repelling one another depending on which poles were nearby. That might explain why the planets moved toward and away from the sun. But then why did they keep moving forward in their orbits? The sun's power seemed somehow to also push them forward. Magnetism didn't lead him to the answer. On to the next analogy.

He eventually decided that planets and stars pulled one another and that larger objects had more pull. That led him to claim—correctly—that the moon influenced tides on Earth. At the time, though, he was mocked for the ridiculous idea of "the moon's dominion over the waters."

Kepler's use of analogies and his thinking traced an incredible journey, from belief that spirits moved the planets in the skies (like just about everyone else at the time) to his realization of the planetary laws of motion, which showed that planets move in predictable paths based on their relation to the sun. Oh, and it also led him to invent astrophysics.

Before Kepler began thinking about these things, there was no concept of gravity as a force. No one had thought of it yet, let alone proved its existence. So he did not have the bene-fit of previous knowledge about universal physical forces. He had no idea about the momentum that keeps the planets in motion. Analogies were all he had. When he published his laws of planetary motion, he called it *A New Astronomy Based upon Causes*. In a time when alchemy—the medieval belief that matter could magically transform—was commonly accepted, Kepler helped usher in the Scientific Revolution. It's clear that he thought outside the box. But what he also did, whenever he was stuck, was to think entirely outside the subject, or domain. He left a trail of records that show his favorite tools for doing that. "I especially love analogies," he wrote. "One should make great use of them."

Kepler's work led him to develop what today are known as Kepler's Laws of Planetary Motion:

> Kepler's First Law: Planets move around the sun in oval-shaped paths called ellipses, with the sun off to one side, not in the center.

> Kepler's Second Law: As a planet orbits the sun, it moves faster when it's closer and slower when it's farther away—but it always sweeps out equal areas in equal amounts of time.

> Kepler's Third Law: Planets that are farther from the sun take more time to go all the way around it.

Mention Johannes Kepler if you want to get psychologist Dedre Gentner excited. She gesticulates. Her tortoiseshell glasses bob up and down. Gentner is probably the world's leading authority on analogical thinking, which is a type of thinking or problem-solving that recognizes similarities among seemingly unrelated ideas or situations. Using analogies and analogical thinking helps people to reason through problems they have never seen before. It takes the new and makes it familiar. Or it takes the familiar and puts it in a new light. A science teacher might explain the basics of how electricity works by comparing it to the way water flows through the pipes in a house, for example. The idea behind analogical thinking is to compare something familiar with something new. "In my opinion," Gentner told me, our ability to think using analogies "is one of the reasons we're running the planet."

But remember that Kepler was facing a problem that wasn't just new to him. The ideas he was trying to reason out were new to all of humanity. There was no previous information for him to use. Kepler had to use analogies to consider the concepts he was working on; there was nothing else to help him think through problems.

Most problems people experience, of course, are not new, so we can rely on comparisons from our own experience. Gentner calls these "surface" analogies. "Most of the time, if you're reminded of things that are similar on the surface, they're going to be relationally similar as well," she explained. Remember how you fixed your tablet when it glitched during a download?

That will probably come to mind when the next glitch occurs.

But the idea that surface analogies can help solve new problems depends on repeating patterns, Gentner told me. Which is "perfectly fine," she said, "if you stay in the same village . . . all your life." But the current world isn't usually as simplified as that. Life today often requires thinking that does not, and sometimes cannot, rely on repeating patterns and previous experience. Like math students who need to figure out the correct strategy to use before they begin to answer a question, everyone needs to be able to pick strategies to solve problems they've never seen before. And we can't just rely on prior experience to choose our strategies. Like Kepler, we have to use analogies to solve problems that might seem different but that have deeper similarities. "In the life we lead today we need to be reminded of things that are only abstractly similar," Gentner told me. "And the more creative you want to be, the more important that is."

Test Your Problem-Solving Skills

In the course of studying problem-solving in the 1930s, Karl Duncker posed one of the most famous hypothetical problems in all of cognitive psychology. Want to give it a try? It goes like this:

Suppose you are a doctor faced with a patient who has a malignant stomach tumor. It is impossible to operate on this patient, but unless the tumor is destroyed the patient will die. There is a kind of ray that can be used to destroy the tumor. If the rays reach the tumor all at once at a sufficiently high intensity, the tumor will be destroyed. Unfortunately, at this intensity the healthy tissue that the rays pass through on the way to the tumor will also be destroyed. At lower intensities the rays are harmless to healthy tissue, but they will not affect the tumor either. What type of procedure might be used to destroy the tumor with the rays and at the same time avoid destroying the healthy tissue?

It's on you to destroy the tumor and save the patient, but the rays are either too powerful or too weak. How can you solve this?

While you're thinking, here's a little story to pass the time: Years ago, a small-town fire chief arrived at a woodshed fire and became concerned that it would spread to a nearby house if it was not extinguished quickly. There was no hydrant nearby, but the shed was next to a lake, so there was plenty of water. Dozens of neighbors were already taking turns with buckets throwing water on the shed, but they weren't making any progress. The neighbors were surprised when the fire chief yelled at them to stop and to all go fill their buckets in the lake. When they returned, the chief arranged them in a circle around the shed and on the count of three had them all throw their water at once. The fire was immediately dampened and soon thereafter extinguished. The town gave the fire chief a pay raise as a reward for quick thinking.

Have you saved your patient yet? If not, don't feel bad. Not many people solve this problem. At least not at first. Only about 10 percent of people solve "Duncker's radiation problem" initially. But the numbers improve when people are presented with both the problem and stories about seemingly unrelated topics, including our fire chief near the lake. People who were given two stories along with the problem and told to use the stories to help them solve the radiation problem "saved" the patient 80 percent of the time.

The answer to the problem, by the way, is that

you (the doctor) could direct multiple low-intensity rays at the tumor from different directions. That would leave healthy tissue intact, but the rays would come together at the tumor site with enough collective intensity to destroy it. Just like how the fire chief arranged neighbors with their buckets around the burning shed so that their water would douse the fire simultaneously.

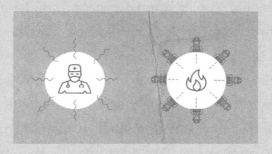

Really, don't feel bad if you didn't get it. In a real experiment you would have taken more time to come up with an answer. But, more to the point, whether you got the right answer or not is unimportant. The important part is what it shows about problem-solving and the usefulness of analogical thinking. Applying a single analogy from an unrelated topic, or different domain, tripled the amount of respondents who solve the radiation problem.

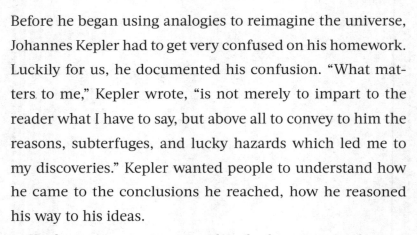

Before he began using analogies to reimagine the universe, Johannes Kepler had to get very confused on his homework. Luckily for us, he documented his confusion. "What matters to me," Kepler wrote, "is not merely to impart to the reader what I have to say, but above all to convey to him the reasons, subterfuges, and lucky hazards which led me to my discoveries." Kepler wanted people to understand how he came to the conclusions he reached, how he reasoned his way to his ideas.

Kepler was a young man when he began to work at an observatory that was on the cutting edge at the time. He was given the assignment nobody wanted: figuring out Mars and its strange orbit. The orbit was known to be a circle, Kepler was told, so he was supposed to figure out why the observations of his boss, Tycho Brahe, didn't show that to be true. Every once in a while, Mars seems to reverse course in the sky—it does a little loop and then carries on in its original direction. Its orbit is not, in fact, circular. At the time, astronomers had proposed all kinds of elaborate reasons to explain how this happened. As usual, Kepler refused to accept their complicated reasons.

He tried asking his peers for help, but his pleas were

ignored. His predecessors had always managed to explain away the deviations of Mars's orbit. Kepler's short Mars assignment (he guessed it would take eight days to solve) turned into five years of calculations trying to describe where Mars appeared in the sky at any given moment. No sooner would he believe he'd done it with great accuracy than he threw his work away. His calculations were close, but not perfect. The imperfection was minuscule. Kepler could assume his model was correct and that something was just slightly off, or he could toss five years of work. He chose to trash his model.

The assignment no one wanted became Kepler's point of entry into a new understanding of the universe. He was in uncharted territory, but he ended up reinventing astronomy by using a lot of analogies.

Kepler's approach to problem-solving turns out to be typical in today's world-class research labs. Psychologist Kevin Dunbar began studying how productive labs work in the 1990s, and what he found was a modern version of Kepler-like thinking. When scientists in top research labs were faced with unexpected results, they treated them not as mistakes but as opportunities to learn or discover something new. And the scientists used analogies to guide them.

When Dunbar started, he simply set out to study and

document the process of discovery in real time. He focused on molecular biology labs because they were doing exciting work, blazing new trails in genetics and treatments for viruses like HIV. He spent more than a year studying labs in the United States, Canada, and Italy, visiting some of the labs every day for months and becoming a familiar and welcome presence to the scientists. On the surface, the labs were very different from one another. One had dozens of members; others were small. A few labs were all men; one was all women. All had excellent reputations around the world.

The weekly lab meetings he attended were the most interesting to Dunbar. Once a week, the entire team came together—lab director, graduate students, technicians, everyone—to discuss some challenge a lab member was facing. The meetings were nothing like the cliché idea of a lonely scientist huddled over their test tubes. Instead, Dunbar saw free-flowing exchanges of ideas. Suggestions were batted back and forth, new experiments were proposed, obstacles discussed. "Those are some of the most creative moments in science," he told me. So he recorded them.

The first fifteen minutes of the meeting were basic business—whose turn it was to order supplies, who had left a mess. Then the action started. Someone presented an unexpected or confusing finding—their version of Kepler struggling with calculating the orbit of Mars. The scientists' first instinct was to blame themselves, wondering if they'd made an error in calculation or in using their equipment. If the unexpected results kept up, the lab accepted them as real, and ideas about what to try and what might be going on would start to fly.

Dunbar witnessed important breakthroughs live and saw that the labs most likely to turn unexpected findings into new knowledge for humanity made a lot of analogies. The labs in which scientists had different professional backgrounds or expertise in various kinds of science were the ones where more, and more varied, analogies were offered during those weekly meetings. And those labs were also where breakthroughs were more reliably produced when the unexpected arose. Those labs were like a modern-day Kepler in group form. They included members with a wide variety of experiences and interests. When the moment came to work with information that puzzled them, they drew on their range of experiences and used analogies—lots of them—to figure things out.

During some lab meetings that Dunbar recorded, a new analogy entered the conversation about every four minutes, and some of them had nothing at all to do with biology.

In one example, Dunbar actually saw two labs encounter the same problem with an experiment at around the same time. Proteins the scientists wanted to measure were getting stuck in a filter, which made them hard to analyze. One of the labs was made up entirely of bacteria experts. The other lab had scientists with chemistry, physics, biology, and genetics backgrounds, as well as medical students. That "lab made an analogy drawing on knowledge from the person with a medical degree, and they figured it out right there at the meeting," Dunbar told me. The lab with only bacteria experts could only draw on their knowledge about bacteria to solve the problem. "That didn't work here, so they had to just start experimenting for weeks to get rid of the problem. It put me in an awkward position because I had seen the answer in another lab's meeting." (As part of the rules of the study, Dunbar was not allowed to share information between labs.)

The study showed that in the face of an unexpected or unfamiliar problem, the range of available analogies had an impact on who learned something new. The lab filled with scientists from diverse backgrounds had access to both more knowledge and more kinds of knowledge and, therefore, to more analogies than the lab with only bacteria experts. That's partly why the more-diverse lab solved the problem much faster.

In the only lab that did not make any new findings during Dunbar's project, everyone had similar and highly specialized backgrounds, and analogies were almost never used. "When all the members of the laboratory have the same knowledge at their disposal, then when a problem arises, a group of similar minded individuals will not provide more information to make analogies than a single individual," Dunbar concluded.

Experts Aren't Always Best

When psychologist and political scientist Philip Tetlock decided to put expert predictions to the test back in 1984, it was after he witnessed a room full of renowned experts confidently and frequently contradict one another. Tetlock decided to study 284 highly educated experts who averaged more than twelve years of experience in their specialties. He collected both short-term and long-term predictions about international politics and economics and analyzed them. His project lasted twenty years and eventually included 82,361 predictions about the future. He found, among other things, that the average expert was a horrific forecaster.

Eventually, in explaining his research and results, Tetlock gave nicknames to two main groups of experts: the narrow-view "hedgehogs"—the ones who "know one big thing"—and the integrator "foxes"—those who "know many little things." Experts who were hedgehogs possessed deep but narrow information. Some had spent their careers studying just a single problem. Their theories about how the world worked were based on the single viewpoint of their specialty. Hedgehogs tended to *burrow* further into their ideas. They were terrible at predicting future political or economic outcomes. Incredibly, the hedgehogs performed especially badly in their areas of expertise, and they actually got worse at making predictions the more educated and more experienced they became in their field.

Foxes, on the other hand, possessed information outside of a single discipline and embodied breadth and range. Tetlock himself is an example of a fox. When I visited his home in Philadelphia and we began a casual conversation, he would start in one direction, then question himself and make an about-face. When a new idea entered the conversation, he was quick to say "Let's say for the sake of argument," which led to him playing out viewpoints from different disciplines or perspectives. He tried on ideas like Instagram filters until it was hard to tell which he actually believed.

After it was published, Tetlock's study caught the attention of the U.S. intelligence community (which includes the CIA and FBI). He eventually helped run a government intelligence project that identified the "foxiest" forecasters as people who were bright and had wide-ranging interests and reading habits but no particular expertise relevant to government intelligence. The best forecasters studied the problem at hand, but they also used outside knowledge and analogies. If they had to make a prediction about a conflict between two countries, they wouldn't only think about those two countries. They might also study other countries that have had conflicts, and businesses that have had conflicts, and even conflicts between individual people. The best forecasters took knowledge from a wide range of sources.

In the second year of the project, volunteers taken from the general public beat experienced intelligence analysts with access to classified data. While it might seem like predicting political and economic outcomes around the world would require narrow specialization, Tetlock showed that it was actually the opposite. Predicting the future is an uncertain matter, which makes wide-ranging thinking crucial.

There is often not much interest in promoting and encouraging range. Nor is there frequently interest in pursuing the kind of knowledge that must be slowly acquired. As we keep seeing, a head start and early, narrow specialization are tempting because they appear to lead to a shorter, more straightforward path to success. But that can be a poor long-term strategy. It's not easy to choose a slow and long route—especially one that may be filled with mistakes and gradual progress—instead. But it's exactly that route that leads to stronger and better learning and that often makes for better problem solvers overall. The scientists who benefited from their varied backgrounds and knowledge to solve their problem in just one meeting would surely agree.

QUESTIONS

1. Johannes Kepler spent five years trying to solve the problem of figuring out the orbit of Mars. He refused to ignore tiny errors in his calculations, and he also refused to accept the popular understanding of the way the universe worked at the time. Do you think the choices he made were easy for him? Why do you think he never gave up?

2. Knowledge isn't limited to the subjects you study in school. What are some topics you know about that aren't school-related? How might your knowledge about those subjects help you the next time you face a tough question in class?

QUESTIONS

3. The next time you join a team or have a group project for school, will you seek out a group of people very similar to you, or will you look for a group that is made up of people with different interests and backgrounds? Why?

PART 3

Creativity:
The More, the Better

6

Gaming the System

Until the mid-nineteenth century, Japan had been a closed and isolated nation that tried to avoid Western cultural influences. For more than two hundred years, rules were in place that banned Japanese citizens from foreign travel and restricted foreign trade, among many other policies. The rules were intended to prevent unwanted Western influence, and they applied even to a certain kind of playing card. Known as hanafuda, or "flower cards," because they had pictures of flowers on them, they were banned because they were associated with gambling and Western culture.

But in the late 1800s, the card ban was finally lifted—which is how it was possible that in the fall of 1889 a young man opened a tiny wooden shop in Kyoto, Japan, to sell playing cards. He hung a sign in the shop's window: "Nintendo."

The precise meaning of the Japanese characters that make up the word "Nintendo" is lost to history. They may have meant "leave luck to heaven" but were more likely a poetic way to say "the company that is allowed to sell hana-fuda." The shop succeeded, and by 1950 the company had a hundred workers, and the founder's twenty-two-year-old great-grandson took over. But trouble was coming. By 1964, Japanese adults were turning to other kinds of gambling, and a bowling craze was contributing to decreased interest in playing cards. So, in a desperate attempt to diversify a company that had survived on hanafuda alone for seventy-five years, the young president began investing in different products. He figured food would never go out of fashion, so he shifted the company to producing instant rice and meals branded with cartoon characters. Then there was a failed taxicab operation. None of it worked, and Nintendo sank into debt. The president resolved to hire top young university graduates to help him innovate.

But Nintendo was a small operation located in Kyoto; the most talented Japanese students wanted to work for big companies in Tokyo, the country's busy capital city. So, by 1965, the president settled for hiring a local electronics graduate named Gunpei Yokoi. Yokoi had struggled through university and received no other job offers.

"What will you do at Nintendo?" Yokoi's classmates asked him. He wasn't worried. "I didn't want to leave Kyoto anyway," he said later. "I never had a specific dream for my work, and it was just fine." (All of Yokoi's ideas and quotations included here are from his own writings and interviews. His works were not published in English, so portions were translated for use in this book.)

His job at Nintendo was to repair and service the playing-card-making machines. There were only a few machines, so Yokoi was the entire maintenance department. He had long been someone who was enthusiastic about his hobbies, which included piano, ballroom dancing, choir, skin diving, model trains, working on cars, and most of all monozukuri—or "thing making." Yokoi was a tinkerer. Before cars came with stereos, he connected a tape recorder to his car radio so he could replay his recordings later either in the car or at home.

In his first few months at Nintendo, there was so little to do that he spent his time tinkering and using company equipment. One day, he cut crisscrossing pieces of wood and built a simple extendable arm. It was similar to the jack-in-the-box kind he had seen in cartoons, the type where a robot's belly opens up and a boxing glove fires out. He added a gripping tool to the outer end, which closed when he squeezed handles to extend the arm. Now he could lazily retrieve distant objects.

The company president saw the new hire goofing around with his contraption and called him into his office. "I thought I would be scolded," Yokoi recalled. Instead, his boss told Yokoi to turn his device into a game. So Yokoi added a group of colored balls that could be grabbed, and the "Ultra Hand" went to market immediately.

It was Nintendo's first toy, and it sold 1.2 million units. The company paid off a chunk of its debt. And that was the end of Yokoi's maintenance career. He was assigned to start Nintendo's first research and development department. Yokoi was going to invent games. The facility that briefly made instant rice was converted into a toy factory.

More toy success followed, but it was a total failure that first year that may have most influenced Yokoi. He helped create Drive Game, a tabletop unit where a player used a steering wheel to guide a plastic car along a racetrack that scrolled beneath the car via electric motor. It was the first Nintendo toy that required electricity. And it was a complete flop. The internal mechanism was advanced for the time, and it ended up being so complex and fragile that it was expensive and hard to produce, and the units were riddled with defects. But the failure planted the seed of a creative approach that Yokoi would hone for the next thirty years.

Yokoi was well aware of his own engineering limitations. As one game-history expert put it, "He studied electronics at a time where the technology was evolving faster than the snow melts in sunlight." Yokoi had no desire (or capability) for Nintendo to compete with electronics companies that were racing one another to invent entirely new technology. Nor could Nintendo compete with Japan's makers of traditional toys.

Instead, with Drive Game in mind, Yokoi decided to put cheap, simple technology to use in ways no one else considered. In the early 1970s, radio-controlled toy cars were popular, but good RC technology was very expensive, so it was a hobby reserved for adults. As he often did, Yokoi thought about a way to make RC toys accessible to more people. He took the tech backward. The more functions an RC toy had, the more radio-control channels it required, and that's what made them expensive. Yokoi stripped the technology down to the absolute bare minimum, which produced a single-channel RC car that could only turn left.

He called his approach to creating the simplified car "lateral thinking with withered technology." The term "lateral thinking" refers to imagining new uses for information—in other words, giving old ideas new purpose by combining ideas that seem to be totally unrelated. "Withered technology" means tech that is old enough to be extremely well understood and easily available. "Withered technology" didn't require a specialist's knowledge. Yokoi had decided that if he could not think more deeply about new technologies, he would think more broadly about old ones. He was intentionally retreating from the cutting edge.

What was the name of the stripped-down RC car that only turned left? Lefty RX, of course. It was less than a tenth the cost of typical RC toys and just fine for counterclockwise races. Even when it did have to navigate obstacles, users easily learned how to left-turn their way out of trouble.

One day in 1977, while riding the high-speed train back from a business trip in Tokyo, Yokoi awoke from a nap and saw a bored passenger playing with a calculator to pass his time on the train. The trend at that time was to make toys as big as possible. But Yokoi wondered, *What if there was*

*a game small enough that it could be played by someone
while they were riding a train?*

He didn't do anything with his idea for a while, until one
day he was asked to fill in as the company president's chauf-
feur. The normal driver had the flu, and, thanks to his interest
in foreign vehicles, Yokoi was the only one at the company
who knew how to drive the president's American Cadillac.
He mentioned his miniature game idea from the front seat.
"He was nodding along," Yokoi recalled, "but he didn't seem
all that interested."

A week later, though, Yokoi received a surprise visit from
company executives at Sharp, a calculator manufacturer. It
turned out that the Nintendo president had been interested
in Yokoi's idea. In fact, he'd shared the idea at the meeting
that Yokoi had driven him to. The president happened to be
sitting next to the head of Sharp and mentioned his chauf-
feur's idea. And Sharp just happened to be eager to find
another use for its LCD screens besides calculators.

Sharp executives weren't convinced it was even possible
to make a display smooth enough for the game Yokoi proposed, which involved a juggler whose arms move left and
right, trying not to drop balls as they speed up. Nonetheless,
the Sharp engineers gave it a try and made Yokoi an LCD
screen in the appropriate size. But then he hit a problem.

The electronics in the tiny game were packed in such a thin space that the liquid crystal display element touched a plate in the screen, which created a visual distortion of light and dark rings.

To fix the distortion problem, Yokoi took an old idea from the credit card industry. Just like how the numbers on some credit cards are raised, Yokoi used old playing-card-printing machines to delicately add hundreds of dots to the screen to keep the plate and the display element separated. As a final flourish, a colleague helped him program a clock into the display. LCD screens were already used in wristwatches, and they figured it would give adults a reason to buy the product they named "Game & Watch."

In 1980, Nintendo released its first three Game & Watch models, hoping to sell one hundred thousand of them. Six hundred thousand copies sold in the first year. Nintendo could not keep up with international demand. Donkey Kong, the familiar gorilla in the Mario franchise, had been introduced in 1981, and when the Donkey Kong Game & Watch was released in 1982, it sold eight million units. Game & Watch remained in production for eleven years and sold 43.4 million units. It also happened to include another Yokoi invention: the directional pad, or "D-pad," which allowed a player to move a character in any direction using just their thumb. After the success of the Game & Watch, Nintendo had another huge success using Yokoi's lateral thinking approach: the company featured the D-pad in the controllers for its revolutionary new Nintendo Entertainment System.

The NES home console brought arcade games into millions of homes around the world and launched a new era of gaming. The combination of Nintendo's two major successes—the Game & Watch and the NES—also led to Yokoi's greatest lateral thinking achievement, a handheld console that played any game a developer could put on a cartridge. It was called the Game Boy.

From a technological standpoint, even in 1989, the Game Boy was laughably basic. Yokoi's team cut every corner. The processor it used had been cutting-edge back in the 1970s. By the mid-1980s, home consoles were in fierce competition over graphics quality. The Game Boy's graphics were truly ugly. It featured a total of four grayscale shades displayed on a tiny screen that was tinted a greenish hue somewhere between mucus and old broccoli. Fast sideways moves appeared smeared across the screen. To top it off, the Game Boy had to compete with handheld consoles from major companies like Sega and Atari that were technologically superior in every way and had color. The Game Boy destroyed them.

And the reason was the Game Boy more than made up

for its old, withered technology with excellent user experience. It was cheap. It could fit in a large pocket. It was all but indestructible. Even if someone managed to drop it and crack the screen—and it had to be a horrific drop—it kept on working. If it were left in a backpack that went in the washing machine, once it dried out it was ready to roll a few days later. Unlike its power-guzzling color competitors, it played for days (or weeks) on AA batteries. Its old hardware was extremely familiar to developers both inside and outside Nintendo, and they pumped out games with amazing speed. *Tetris*, *Super Mario Land*, *The Final Fantasy Legend*, and a ton of sports games were released in the first year. All were smash hits. The game-programming community loved the Game Boy's simple technology. The Game Boy sold 118.7 million units; it was far and away the bestselling console of the twentieth century.

Even though he was enormously successful by then, Yokoi had to fight for his "lateral thinking with withered technology" concept to be approved for the Game Boy. "It was difficult to get Nintendo to understand," he said later. Yokoi was convinced, though, that if users were drawn into the games, technological power would be an afterthought. "If you draw two circles on a blackboard, and say, 'That's a snowman,' everyone who sees it will sense the white color of the snow," he argued. Yokoi succeeded because he knew he could use old technology in creative new ways. That might sound simple, but it's actually a rare mode of thinking.

People have a well-documented tendency to consider only familiar uses for objects. The most famous example is the "candle problem," in which participants are given a candle, a box of tacks, and a book of matches and told to attach the candle to the wall so that wax doesn't drip on the table below. Solvers may try to melt the candle to the wall or tack it up somehow, neither of which work. When the problem is presented with the tacks outside of their box, solvers are more likely to think of the empty box as a potential candle holder and to solve the problem by tacking the box to the wall and placing the candle inside it. For Yokoi, the tacks were always outside the box. He was always looking for new ways to use familiar things.

Unquestionably, Yokoi needed narrow specialists. And he was the first to admit it. "I don't have any particular specialist skills," he once said. "I have a sort of vague knowledge of everything."

But he advised young employees not just to play with technology but to play with ideas. "Everyone takes the approach of learning detailed, complex skills. If no one did this then there wouldn't be people who shine as engineers . . .

Looking at me, from the engineer's perspective, it's like, 'Look at this idiot,' but once you've got a couple hit products under your belt, this word 'idiot' seems to slip away somewhere." He understood the importance of narrow specialists, but he also encouraged them to tinker.

He spread his philosophy as his team grew and asked everyone to consider alternate uses for old technology. He realized that he had been fortunate to be hired by a playing-card company rather than an established toy and game maker. His ideas were not rejected because of his technical limitations. As the company flourished, he worried that young engineers would be too concerned about looking stupid to share ideas for novel uses of old technology, so he began intentionally blurting out crazy ideas at meetings to set the tone. "Once a young person starts saying things like, 'Well, it's not really my place to say . . . ' then it's all over," he said.

Yokoi's greatest failure came when he departed from his own philosophy of using old technology in new ways. One of his last Nintendo projects was the Virtual Boy, a gaming headset that used new, experimental technology. It was a device that sat on a table and required the user to assume a strange posture to see the screen. The Virtual Boy was ahead of its time, but nobody bought it.

Tragically, Yokoi died in a traffic accident in 1997. But his philosophy of lateral thinking survived. In 2006, Nintendo's president said that the Nintendo Wii game console was a direct outgrowth of Yokoi's approach. The Wii used extremely simple games and technology from a previous console, but it had motion-based controls that were a literal game changer. The Nintendo Switch, too, doesn't use very powerful or new processors, but wields limited tech in creative ways—and it still uses the D-pad!

Given its basic hardware, the Wii was criticized as not innovative. But a Harvard professor argued that it was actually the most important kind of innovation, an "empowering innovation"—one that makes technology more widely available, creating both new customers and new jobs. Yokoi's way of thinking brought video games to an entirely new audience.

QUESTIONS

1. Is there a subject you know a lot about and that you are an expert or specialized thinker in? How might you try using that expertise in a different way? How might you apply it to an unrelated challenge or area?

2. How might the story of Nintendo have been different if Yokoi had not been a tinkerer who played around with company equipment when he was bored? Do you think Nintendo would have become a gaming company anyway?

QUESTIONS

3. Can you think of anything that you play with or use that utilizes older technology? What makes that device still fun to play with or useful in a world of touch screens? How might that aspect be incorporated into new technology to improve the experience?

7

Broad Strokes

Inventor Andy Ouderkirk never meant to create a new kind of glitter. He laughed as he recalled the story. "It was with three gentlemen who owned the company, and I'll just forever remember them holding up a vial and just looking at me and saying, 'This is a breakthrough in glitter.' "

As it turns out, standard glitter just sparkles; this glitter blazed, as if the vial held a colony of magical fireflies. Ouderkirk had envisioned a lot of applications for the material he invented. But glitter wasn't one of them. It came as a pleasant surprise. "Here I am, a physical chemist," he told me. "I usually think of breakthroughs as being very sophisticated advanced technologies."

Andy Ouderkirk was an inventor at the Minnesota-based company 3M, maker of Post-it Notes, adhesive tape, and many other everyday products. Andy was one of twenty-eight "corporate scientists," the highest title among the company's sixty-five hundred scientists and engineers. His road to breakthrough glitter began when he attempted to challenge a two-hundred-year-old principle of physics known as Brewster's law, which had been interpreted to mean that no surface could reflect light near perfectly at every angle.

Andy wondered if he could create a highly reflective film by layering many thin plastic surfaces on top of one another. A group of specialists he consulted assured him it could not be done, which was exactly what he wanted to hear. "If they say, 'It's a great idea, go for it, makes sense,' what is the chance you're the first person to come up with it? Precisely zero," he told me.

In fact, he was certain it was physically possible, because Mother Nature offered evidence that it was. The iridescent-blue morpho butterfly, for example, has no blue pigment whatsoever. Its wings glow azure and sapphire from thin layers of scales that bend and reflect particular wavelengths of blue light. There were more examples too. The plastic of a water bottle bends, or refracts, light differently depending on the light's angle. "It's in front of you literally every day," Ouderkirk said of the concept. "But nobody ever thought of making optical films out of this."

He formed a small team that accomplished just that. And the uses of the invention that was supposed to be impossible went well beyond glitter. Inside cell phones and laptops, Ouderkirk's film drastically reduces the power needed to keep screens bright. It improves efficiency in LED light bulbs and solar panels. It enhanced the energy efficiency of a projector so dramatically that it only needed a tiny battery for bright video.

Ouderkirk was named the 2013 *R&D Magazine* Innovator of the Year, and over his three decades working at 3M he played a role in hundreds of inventions. Along the way, he became fascinated with the ingredients of invention, inventive teams, and individual inventors themselves. Eventually, he decided to research them.

Ouderkirk and two other researchers who set out to study inventors at 3M wanted to know what kind of inventor made the greatest contributions. They found both specialized inventors who focused on a single technology and generalist inventors who were not leading experts in anything but had worked across numerous areas.

The specialists and the generalists, they found, both made

contributions, and one group was not superior to the other. The specialists were good at working for a long time on difficult technical problems and anticipating obstacles. The generalists tended to get bored working in one area for too long. They added value by taking technology from one area and applying it in others.

Ouderkirk's study uncovered one more type of inventor. These inventors had broad experience and also at least one area of depth. Ouderkirk is an example of this kind of inventor. He had been interested in chemistry since his second-grade teacher showed off a model volcano eruption. He took a winding path, from community college to a chemistry PhD to working completely outside of his background area when he arrived at 3M. "What nobody ever told me in my whole career," he said, is that it's good to be an expert, "but it's also good to know a little bit about everything else."

In his first eight years at 3M, Ouderkirk worked with more than one hundred different teams. Nobody handed him important projects with enormous potential impact, but his breadth of knowledge helped him identify them. "If you're working on well-defined and well-understood problems, specialists work very, very well," he told me. "As ambiguity and uncertainty increases . . . breadth becomes increasingly important."

Specialization is obvious: keep going straight. Breadth is trickier to grow, and maybe trickier to assess. Professors Alva Taylor and Henrich Greve decided to study the creative impact of individual breadth and chose what might be a surprising area to focus on: comic books.

More than fifty years ago, in 1971, the U.S. Department of Health, Education, and Welfare asked Marvel Comics editor in chief Stan Lee to create a story that educated readers about drug abuse. Lee wrote a Spider-Man narrative in which Peter Parker's best friend overdoses on pills. The Comics Code Authority, the industry's own censorship organization, did not approve of it. Marvel published it anyway. It was received so well that censorship standards were immediately updated, and the creative comic book story floodgates swung open. Comics creators developed superheroes with complex emotional problems. Graphic novels began to win major literary prizes. And readers benefited from diverse characters and stories.

In their study, Taylor and Greve tracked individual creators' careers, and they analyzed the commercial value of thousands of comic books. They expected to find that creators learned by repetition and that creators making more comics in a certain amount of time would make better comics on average. They were wrong.

They found that amount of experience had no impact at all on the commercial success of comics. So, what helped creators make better comics on average? And what helped them innovate with new styles of comics?

There are twenty-two different genres, or categories, of comic books, from comedy to crime to nonfiction to sci-fi. The answer to what helped creators make better comics depended on how many of those twenty-two genres a creator had worked in. Length of experience did not set creators apart, but the breadth of their experience did. Broad genre experience made creators better on average and more likely to innovate. And, on top of that, an individual creator who had worked in four or more genres was found to be more innovative than a team of creators who only had experience in the same number of genres.

Taylor and Greve titled their study "Superman or the Fantastic Four? Knowledge Combination and Experience in Innovative Teams." "When seeking innovation in knowledge-based industries," they wrote, "it is best to find one 'super' individual. If no individual with the necessary combination of diverse knowledge is available, one should form a 'fantastic' team."

That finding immediately reminded me of my own favorite comics creators. Japanese comics and animated-film creator Hayao Miyazaki may be best known for the dreamlike epic

Spirited Away, but his comics and animation career before that left almost no genre untouched. He ranged from pure fantasy and fairy tales to historical fiction, sci-fi, slapstick comedy, illustrated historical essays, action-adventure, and much more.

Jordan Peele is not a comics creator, but the writer and first-time director of the extraordinarily unique surprise hit *Get Out* struck a similar note when he credited comedy writing for his skill at timing information reveals in a horror film.

"Some tools work fantastically in certain situations, advancing technology in smaller but important ways, and those tools are well known and well practiced," Andy Ouderkirk told me. But he also pointed out that "those same tools will also pull you away from a breakthrough innovation." The point is that even in extremely specialized areas of cutting-edge technology, the most effective experts have broad experience and skills.

A Broad Network

Charles Darwin, the British scientist best known for his theory of evolution and his book *On the Origin of Species*, "could be considered a professional outsider," according to cre-ativity researcher Dean Keith Simonton. Darwin was not associated with a university, nor was he a professional scientist at any institution. Instead, he made many friends and acquaintances in the scientific community who he could learn from. For a time, he focused narrowly on barnacles but got so tired of it that he declared, "I am unwilling to spend more time on the subject." When Darwin got bored sticking in one area, that was that.

For his influential contributions to the study of evolution, Darwin's broad network was crucial. Darwin always juggled multiple projects and had more than 200 scientific pen pals who can be grouped roughly into thirteen broad themes based on his various interests. He peppered these correspondents with questions. He cut up their letters to paste pieces of information from them in his own notebooks. Howard Gruber, who studied Darwin's journals, described the pages this way: "ideas tumble over each other in a seemingly chaotic fashion." When his chaotic notebooks became too hard to manage, Darwin tore pages out and filed them by theme. Just for his experiments with seeds, he exchanged letters with geologists, botanists, ornithologists, and conchologists in France, South Africa, the United States, the Azores, Jamaica, and Norway, not to mention a number of amateur naturalists and some gardeners he happened to know. "In some respects," Gruber wrote, "Charles Darwin's greatest works represent interpretative compilations of facts first gathered by others." In other words, Darwin can be viewed as a great example of a generalist who put his broad network of other experts to excellent use.

Professor Abbie Griffin has made it her work to study people like Andy Ouderkirk—modern-day inventors and tinkerers—"serial innovators," she and two colleagues termed them. He was, in fact, in one of her studies. The findings about who these people are should sound familiar by now. Griffin's study found that tinkerers "appear to flit among ideas" and have a "broad range of interests." These innovators "read more (and more broadly) than other technologists and have a wider range of outside interests." They have a strong desire to "learn significantly across multiple domains." Griffin also found that serial innovators have a need to communicate with people who have technical expertise that differs from their own.

Toward the end of their book *Serial Innovators*, Griffin and her coauthors offer some advice to anyone responsible for hiring new employees at a company. They recognize that serial innovators may not seem like strong job candidates and that their wide breadth of interests may not neatly match company expectations or standard hiring requirements. But Griffin suggests that the people in charge of hiring should seek out serial innovators. "Look for wide-ranging interests," she and her coauthors advise. "Look for multiple hobbies." One serial innovator you may have heard of, *Hamilton* creator Lin-Manuel Miranda, described his broad thinking this way: "I have a lot of apps open in my brain right now."

As we've seen, breadth of experience is invaluable, and narrow specialization can be remarkably efficient. The challenge is understanding how crucial both are for success.

QUESTIONS

1. Why do you think Andy Ouderkirk was glad to be told that his idea for creating a highly reflective film was impossible? Has anyone ever told you that something couldn't be done, but you tried anyway?

2. Comic book creators who work on stories across many different categories tend to be more successful than those who stick to creating only one kind of story. Do you tend to stick with what's familiar? How might you broaden your experience, whether it's a creative writing assignment, an after-school activity, or trying a new food?

QUESTIONS

3. Think about the generalists and serial innovators discussed in this chapter. Why do you think that working across fields is a strength? Can you think of any times you were working on a problem at school or with your friends when an unexpected or unusual solution saved the day?

PART 4

Playing:
Keep It Up

8

Recess for Your Brain

Scientist Oliver Smithies was in the lab as usual that day. It was a Saturday in 1954, which meant he was doing his "Saturday-morning experiments," as Oliver called them. Nobody was around, and he felt free from the normal rules of his scientific work. On Saturday, he didn't have to weigh things carefully. He could take a pinch of this and a dash of that for an experiment that during the week would be considered a waste of time and equipment. He could try something that intrigued him but had little to do with his professional work. One needs to let the brain think about something different from its daily work, he would say. "On Saturday," as Oliver put it, "you don't have to be completely rational."

Oliver worked in a lab studying insulin, the hormone that helps move sugar from your blood into your cells, so your body can use it for energy or store it for later. Oliver was trying to separate the molecules on a special kind of paper so he could study them, but they kept sticking to the paper instead of separating. Oliver had heard that a local children's hospital used starch grains instead of paper to solve the stickiness. He knew he could try that, but then he'd have to slice each individual grain of starch into fifty pieces and analyze each one individually. It would take forever.

Then Oliver remembered something from when he was twelve. He grew up in the town of Halifax in England and would watch his mother iron his father's work shirts. She used starch to make the shirt collars stiff. She dipped each shirt in gooey, hot starch and then ironed it. It had been Oliver's job to dispose of the starch when she was finished. In his lab that Saturday, he remembered that when it cooled, the liquid starch congealed into a soft, jelly-like consistency. Aha!

Thinking about that cooled, thickened starch, Oliver went around his lab's building, raiding supply closets for starch grains. He cooked the grains, let them cool into a gel, and tried again with the sticky insulin molecules. "Very promising!" his notebook page from that day reads. Oliver's work was the start of a process that eventually would revolutionize biology and chemistry.

When I spoke with Oliver Smithies in 2016, he was ninety years old and still in his lab. It was a Saturday. He was thinking about how the kidney separates large and small molecules. "At the moment, it's a Saturday-morning theoretical experiment," he said.

What struck me as Smithies spoke was his joy in experimentation—not just in his lab but in his life. He was an example of many of the ideas I set out to explore in this book. From the outside, he looked like a true narrow specialist. He was a molecular biochemist, after all, a scientist who studies chemical processes in living organisms at a molecular level. Except that being a molecular biochemist wasn't really a job someone could train for at the time Smithies was a student. The field was very much still developing. Instead, he studied medicine, until he attended a talk by a professor who was combining chemistry and biology. "He lectured about this new subject, which hadn't yet been invented, in a sense," Smithies told me. "It was marvelous, and I thought, 'I'd like to do that. I'd better learn some chemistry.' "

Just like that, he switched to studying chemistry. He never even worried that he might be behind others in the field. On the contrary, "that was really very valuable, because at the end I had a good background in biology and wasn't frightened of biology, and then I wasn't frightened of chemistry. That gave me a great deal of power in the early days of molecular biology." So his job title, molecular biochemist—which sounds like it requires hyper-specialization—was actually a bold blend of two separate fields when Smithies started out.

Smithies was a professor at the University of North Carolina when we spoke in 2016. He passed away nine months later, at ninety-one. To the end of his life, he encouraged students to think and live broadly and to make their own paths to find the best match for their interests. "Take your skills to a place that's not doing the same sort of thing," he said he told his students. "Take your skills and apply them to a new problem, or take your problem and try completely new skills."

Smithies lived the advice he gave. When he was in his fifties, he switched to learning how to work with DNA. He was awarded the Nobel Prize in Physiology or Medicine in 2007 for his work in figuring out how to modify disease-causing genes so that they could be studied in animals. To other scientists, that makes him a very late specializer.

Over his career, Oliver filled and kept 150 notebooks. As he walked me through important pages, he kept repeating, "That was also Saturday." When I pointed it out, he replied, "Well, I've had people say, 'Why did you come to work any other day!'"

His breakthroughs, of course, were the exceptions. Not all of his work went on to win Nobel Prizes. One Saturday-morning experiment accidentally dissolved an important piece of equipment. During another, Oliver contaminated his shoes with a putrid chemical. He thought he had aired them out well enough until he heard an elderly woman ask another if she smelled a dead body. Oliver could not resist "picking up anything" to experiment with, he said, a habit his colleagues noticed. Rather than throw out damaged equipment, they would leave it for him, with the label *NBGBOKFO*: "no bloody good, but OK for Oliver." They knew he'd find some new use for it.

An enthusiastic, playful streak shows up frequently in research on creative thinkers. Art historian Sarah Lewis studies creative achievement and has described the mindsets of some people she's studied as "deliberate amateur." The word "amateur," Lewis points out, was not originally an insult. It comes from the Latin word for a person who adores a particular endeavor. "Breakthroughs often occur when you start down a road, but wander off for a ways and pretend as if you have just begun," Lewis wrote. Like Vincent van Gogh or Frances Hesselbein or plenty of young athletes, even creative scientists can look from the outside like they are behind, until all of a sudden they very much aren't.

At some point we all specialize in one way or another, whether it's deciding to focus only on playing your favorite sport or choosing exactly which field of science you study someday. Because we all eventually specialize somehow, the rush to do it can seem logical. Fortunately, there are a lot of people out there who are working to de-emphasize the importance of having a head start. These people want us to have it all—the creative power that broad experience provides and the deep experience of specialization and expertise. Some believe the future of discovery and innovation depends on it.

In 1945, Vannevar Bush, the man who had overseen U.S. military science during World War II, wrote a report at the request of President Franklin Delano Roosevelt in which he explained successful innovation culture. The report was titled *Science—the Endless Frontier*, and it led to the creation of the National Science Foundation. That organization supported three generations of wildly successful scientific discovery, from Doppler radar, which helps meteorologists predict the weather, to web browsers. "Scientific progress on a broad front results from the free play of free intellects, working on subjects of their own choice," Bush wrote, "in the manner dictated by their curiosity for exploration of the unknown." Bush likely would have been a big supporter of Smithies's Saturday experiments, if he'd been aware of them.

A curious phenomenon has appeared in recent years almost each time the Nobel Prizes are awarded. In their acceptance speech, a person getting the famous award explains that they didn't know what they would find when they started experimenting. They worry that their work couldn't be done today because there's so much pressure to show results quickly rather than taking time to explore. As the 2016 Nobel laureate Yoshinori Ohsumi, a Japanese biologist, said in his Nobel lecture, "truly original discoveries in science are often triggered by unpredictable and unforeseen small findings . . . Scientists are increasingly required to provide evidence of immediate and tangible applications of their work." He meant that scientists have to pursue such narrowly specialized goals and be so hyper-efficient that they're able to say what they will find before they look for it. That's hyper-specialization in the extreme.

Leading scientists understand that the point of their work, their end goal, is to find useful applications for it in the real world, but the question we need to consider is how best to get there. "Free play" when it comes to intellect and innovation sounds horribly inefficient. But is it?

Developing soccer players who spend time just shooting around on the field instead of drilling on specific skills may look disorganized and unfocused—at first. But when someone actually takes the time to study how breakthroughs occur, or, for example, how the players on Germany's 2014 World Cup–winning team developed their soccer skills when they were younger, the value of free play is clear. The championship team was found to have players who "performed less organized practice . . . but greater proportions of playing activities." In other words, fewer drills and more free play helped make them champs.

At its core, hyper-specialization is a well-meaning drive for efficiency—the best and fastest approach to developing a sports skill, or to learning to play an instrument, or to working on a new technology. But the wisdom of only pursuing laser-focused, efficient development is limited. Inefficiency needs to be promoted too. Because when you allow yourself time to daydream or brainstorm and to share ideas with other people, it allows you to make connections and discoveries that might otherwise be missed—or never happen at all.

QUESTIONS

1. What's your favorite activity or hobby? What do you like about it? When is the last time you did it just for fun?

2. Do you do any activities where you experiment with new ideas or techniques? Why do you think experimenting can be both fun and beneficial for performance?

3. Do you know what you want to be when you grow up? Do you think it might change in the future?

9

Range Widely

When I began to write and speak about the data that indicate athletes who go on to reach the elite level are usually not early specializers, the reactions (particularly from parents) reliably fell into two categories: (1) simple disbelief, as in, "That can't be true!" and (2) "So, in one sentence, what is the advice?"

How could I explain in a single sentence how crucial it is to embrace broad experience and the journey of experimentation if you want to have success like Roger Federer or Frances Hesselbein or Oliver Smithies, just to name a few

examples of the many we've read about? Especially if you
want to arrive at a place that is exactly right just for you. Like
the paths of those people, my own exploration of breadth
and specialization was inefficient. What began as a search
for one sentence of advice for parents ended in this book.

Stories of innovation and self-discovery *can* look like orderly journeys from A to B. Sort of like how on the surface
inspirational accounts of the journeys of elite athletes appear
straightforward. But the stories usually get murkier when
they're examined in depth or over time. The popular concept of the Tiger Woods path minimizes the role of detours,
breadth, and experimentation. It is appealing because it is a
tidy tale, low on uncertainty and high on efficiency. After all,
who doesn't like a head start? Experimentation is not neat,
but it is common, and it has advantages, and it requires more
than the typical tolerance for failure.

Range in the Real World

I had just written a book about genetics and
athleticism when I received an email from someone named Jill Viles. Jill explained that she was
a thirty-nine-year-old woman from Iowa, and a

muscular dystrophy patient. Muscular dystrophy is a genetic disease that causes muscles to become increasingly weaker. Jill was not a typical muscular dystrophy patient, and the doctors and scientists who treated her had been unable to figure out exactly what was wrong with her. Jill was determined to figure it out herself. She read medical journals, talked to a wide variety of experts, interned in a lab, studied her own family, and educated herself in any way she could. Eventually, she learned what nobody else had figured out: that she had not one but *two* rare diseases. In addition to muscular dystrophy, she has lipodystrophy, which causes the fat on her body to disappear. Jill had learned so much that one day when she was looking at a picture of one of the best sprinters in the world, she immediately decided that she and the sprinter had a special connection. Unlike Jill, the sprinter, a Canadian Olympic medalist named Priscilla Lopes-Schliep, had enormous muscles, but—just like Jill—she was also missing fat around her muscles. By the time Jill emailed me, she had a full theory: that she and Priscilla had the same mutated gene, but because Priscilla doesn't have muscular dystrophy, her body had found some way to "go around it," as Jill put it. It was clear to me that Jill had done her homework.

If her theory was right, Jill hoped that scientists would study her and Priscilla to figure out how to help people with muscles like Jill's. She wanted my help convincing Priscilla to get a genetic test. I was very skeptical at first, as was an expert I consulted. It took time for Jill to convince me that because of her unique life experience, she could see something that no specialist could. Eventually, I did help connect Jill to Priscilla. When they met in person, Priscilla recalled thinking, "There is something real here. Let's research. Let's find out." It would take a year to find a doctor willing to analyze Priscilla's genome.

In the end, tests and analysis showed that Jill was right. She and Priscilla did have a mutation on the same gene. And not only that, but the tests had revealed that Priscilla was in need of medical treatment for an undiagnosed condition. Jill's research and determination, and her understanding about her own body, had led to a life-altering medical treatment for a professional athlete.

Without Jill, Priscilla's health may have suffered.

"I can understand a patient can learn more about their disease," Dr. Abhimanyu Garg, the doctor who'd done the genetic analysis at Jill's request, told me. "But to reach out to someone else, and figure out their problem also. It is a remarkable feat."

Creativity researcher Dean Keith Simonton has shown that the more work successful creators produced, the more failures they churned out, and the higher their chances of extreme success. Thomas Edison held more than a thousand patents, most for inventions that were completely unimportant. And he was rejected for many more. His failures were many, but his successes—the mass-market light bulb, the phonograph, a precursor to the film projector—were earthshaking.

Or take William Shakespeare. Sandwiched between the enduring classics *King Lear* and *Macbeth*, the playwright quilled *Timon of Athens*, which is not usually remembered as a greatest hit.

Sculptor Rachel Whiteread was the first woman ever to win the Turner Prize—a British award for the best artistic production of the year. She also received a one-time "anti-Turner Prize" for the worst British artist. She won both awards in the same year.

And in the same year that actress Sandra Bullock won the Academy Award for Best Actress for her role in the hit football movie *The Blind Side*, she also "won" an award known as a Razzie, which playfully recognizes the worst contributions to the movies each year, for her role in *All About Steve*. Actually, Bullock received two Razzies for that movie: Worst Actress and Worst Screen Couple.

When I was researching the history of video games to write about Nintendo, I learned that a man named Howard Scott Warshaw, who is now a psychotherapist, was once an Atari video game designer. He used extremely limited technology to make a sci-fi game named *Yars' Revenge*. It was the bestselling original title for Atari's 2600 console during the early 1980s, when Atari became the fastest-growing company in U.S. history. The same year he created *Yars' Revenge*, Warshaw designed the Atari adaptation of the hit film *E.T.* Again, he experimented with limited technology. This time, the game flopped so badly that it was pronounced the biggest commercial failure in video game history. It was blamed for the near-overnight demise of the entire company and led to the legendary story of the "Great Video Game Burial of 1983." The legend held that Atari buried millions of copies of the game in a landfill in New Mexico. In 2014, the site was excavated as part of a documentary. It actually did contain buried copies of *E.T.*, but definitely not millions.

And that's how it goes on the disorderly path of experimentation. Original creators tend to strike out a lot, but they also hit mega grand slams. A baseball comparison doesn't really do it justice, though. Because, as business writer Michael Simmons put it, in baseball, "when you swing, no matter how well you connect with the ball, the most runs you can get is four." In the wider world, "every once in a while, when you step up to the plate, you can score 1,000 runs." It doesn't mean breakthrough creation is luck—although that helps—but rather that it is hard and inconsistent. Going where no one ever has means there is no well-defined formula or perfect system to follow. The fact is, if you want the sky highs, you have to be willing to tolerate a lot of lows.

Scientist Dashun Wang has studied what he calls "hot streaks" in people's jobs—when they produce a string of their best work in a row. Wang found that hot streaks tend to happen after a period of experimentation or exploration.

"Our data shows that people ought to explore a bunch of things" and then decide what's the best fit for them, Wang said. As journalist Derek Thompson explained in an article about Wang's work, "This precise sequence—exploration, followed by exploitation—was the single best predictor of the onset of a hot streak." Within Wang's study, which looked at thousands of scientists, film directors, and artists, the term "exploitation" means taking something important that you learned during your period of exploration and then putting it to use in your work.

In this book I've tried to explain the power of and encourage broad, diverse experience and exploration of new activities and ideas in a world that increasingly demands hyper-specialization and that would have you decide what you should be before first figuring out who you are.

Early on, I discussed athletes and musicians because they are often identified today with early specialization. But among athletes who go on to compete at the elite level, broad early experience and delayed specialization are the norm. Musicians arrive at greatness from a wide array of paths, and early hyper-specialization is often not necessary for skill development. Sviatoslav Richter was one of the greatest pianists of the twentieth century. He didn't start formal lessons until he was twenty-two years old. Steve Nash is a relatively normal-sized Canadian who did not get a basketball until he was thirteen years old; he won the National Basketball Association's Most Valuable Player award twice. As I write this, I am listening to a professional violinist who only started playing when she was eighteen. Of course, she was told to stop before she even started because she was too old. She now makes a point of teaching beginner adults.

So, to answer that request for one sentence of advice? *Don't feel behind.* Two Roman historians recorded that when Julius Caesar was a young man he saw a statue of Alexander the Great in Spain and broke down in tears. "Alexander at my age had conquered so many nations, and I have all this time done nothing that is memorable," he supposedly said. Pretty soon after that, his worry was a distant memory, and Caesar was in charge of the Roman Republic—which he turned into a dictatorship before he was murdered by his own pals. It's fair to say that, like a lot of young athletes, he peaked early.

Compare yourself to yourself yesterday, not to other people who aren't you. Everyone progresses at a different rate, so don't let anyone else make you feel behind. You probably don't even know where exactly you're going, so feeling behind doesn't help. Instead, start planning your own experiments that you can learn from, maybe your own personal version of Smithies's Saturday-morning experiments.

Approach your own personal journey like Michelangelo approached a block of marble. He was willing to learn and adjust as he went, and even to abandon a project if things went really wrong. You should be just as willing to revise a previous goal or change directions entirely should the need arise. As we have seen, research on creators in areas from technological innovation to comic books shows the value of broad experience. Even when you move on from an area, the experience you gained from it is not wasted.

Finally, remember that there is nothing wrong with specialization. We all specialize to one degree or another at some point along the way. My initial spark of interest in this topic came from reading articles and watching speeches that treated early hyper-specialization as some sort of life hack or shortcut that will save you from wasting your time seeking out diverse experiences and experimentation. I hope I have added ideas to that discussion, because plenty of research suggests that personal experimentation is a source of power and that head starts are overrated. As Supreme Court Justice Oliver Wendell Holmes wrote a century ago about the free exchange of ideas, "it is an experiment, as all life is an experiment."

QUESTIONS

1. Have you ever witnessed someone you know—or a team you cheer for—have a hot streak? What do you think indicates when a hot streak is happening?

2. Deciding it's time to switch activities or give up a hobby isn't always easy. How might the information you've read in this book affect your thinking?

3. It's hard not to constantly compare yourself to other people, both in your life and online. How might you try, instead, to focus on comparing yourself now to yourself a week ago, or a month ago, or a year ago, so that you can focus on your own progress?

QUESTIONS

4. We've seen that giving up on something isn't as simple as just quitting; it opens up opportunities to try something else. Have you ever wanted to quit something but decided not to? How might things have turned out differently if you had not stuck with it?

Afterword

Not long after the original edition of *Range* was first published in 2019, I faced tennis legend Serena Williams. Not on a court, thankfully, but in a conference room. I was onstage, giving a talk about some of the research in this book. She was in the second row, right of center.

On one hand, this was exhilarating. The publication of *Range* had led me to opportunities like speaking in front of an audience that included Serena Williams. On the other hand, it was terrifying.

I was confident in the evidence I planned to present that day, which would show, among other things, that when they are children, future elite athletes tend to do a wider variety of activities than their peers. But, as far as I knew, Serena's upbringing was the definition of early specialization. The exact opposite of what I was about to share. A person can present all the evidence and research in the world; if the G.O.A.T. stands up after the talk and says you're an idiot, it's going to be a bad day.

I went ahead with my talk, explaining the benefits of not specializing, and finished with a nervous joke: Does anyone other than Serena Williams have a question? But, of course, Serena raised her hand. As it turned out, she didn't really have a question.

"I think my father was ahead of his time," she said. She then shared with the audience that she had participated in ballet, gymnastics, tae kwon do, and track and field. I had been a senior writer at *Sports Illustrated*, but I had never heard any of those details. When I spoke with her one-on-one later in the day, she mentioned that she and her sister Venus would throw a football to develop the motion for a powerful serve. She also said that their father took them off the junior travel circuit at one point so they could focus on school.

And, as we've seen, Serena and Venus Williams weren't alone. The science shows—over and over—that tales about avoiding early specialization don't apply only in the world of elite sports. Taking the time to explore, whether it's trying new solutions or ideas or seeking new knowledge or skills, is incredibly beneficial.

Shortly after the original edition of *Range* came out, Ruth

Brennan Morrey—a former college soccer co-captain, pro triathlete, and psychology PhD—tagged me on social media: "Listening to @DavidEpstein 'Range' in the car with 12 year old daughter. 'Mom, why do we make "What I want to be when I grow up" signs on the first day of school? We should make "Top 5 things I want to learn about this year" signs.' Smart cookie. :-)" Indeed she is.

As psychologist Angela Duckworth wrote just when *Range* was first being published, it is neither "necessary nor healthy" for young people to be directed toward one career before they can make that decision for themselves. Instead, she wrote encouragingly about "a young child who decides today that she wants to become a doctor but thinks tomorrow that she'd rather build houses. A teenager who decides, no, she won't go out for track this year and instead will see what it's like to write for the school newspaper." Specialization has its benefits, she added, "but before specialization comes sampling, the exploration of possibilities that, really, you cannot know anything about until you try them." Her words are important to remember, especially if well-meaning adults urge you to stick with a sport even if you feel finished with it, or if they suggest it's better to commit to the same activity or club year after year. The concept of finding good match quality through experimenting may be unfamiliar, but it is worth considering now that you're aware of it.

While many of the stories in *Range* portray uncommon achievements, they are intended to serve as reminders that the research I've discussed absolutely applies to a much broader part of the population—including you. In fact, a major theme of this book aligns with international research that found that sometimes the actions that provide a head start will undermine long-term development, whether that is learning new material or developing a skill. I think we need to be aware of how easy it is to be fooled by head starts. Hopefully some of the stories from this book—from the artist Titus Kephar to the inventor of the Nintendo Game Boy, Gunpei Yokoi—might come to mind when more popular Tiger Woods–type stories surface. It could add much-needed balance to how we consider the topic of head starts.

Because the question of how broad or specialized to be is important to just about everyone at some point or another. And, like any complex question that involves human beings, there is no one-size-fits-all answer. My goal is to make discussions about this crucial topic more interesting and useful.

—David Epstein

April 2024

FIVE THINGS I WANT TO LEARN ABOUT THIS YEAR

1.

2.

3.

4.

5.

Discovering Your Range: Ask an Adult

As you're discovering your own skills and exploring your interests, consider asking an adult in your life the following questions:

1. How many different jobs have you worked in?

2. Did you always expect to be doing what you're currently doing in life?

3. Is there something that happened in your life that turned out very differently than you expected?

4. Is there something you've learned about yourself through your work that you didn't know before?

5. What's something important that you care about now that you wouldn't have expected when you were younger?

Glossary

Analogical thinking: A type of thinking or problem-solving that recognizes similarities among seemingly unrelated ideas or situations.

Blocked practice: Practicing the same type of problem over and over.

Deliberate practice: Repetitive practice at one specific or specialized skill, with little deviation, focused on error correction.

Desirable difficulties: The concept that even though an obstacle makes learning more challenging, slower, and more frustrating in the short term, it actually results in better learning in the long term.

Durable learning: Long-lasting learning students will retain.

Early or narrow specialization: Choosing one skill or sport to focus on developing as soon as possible, to the exclusion of all others.

Flexible learning: Learning that can be applied broadly.

Generation effect: The idea that struggling to come up with—or to generate—an answer on your own, even if you come up with the wrong answer, enhances the learning process.

Innovation: The introduction of new ideas and methods.

Lateral thinking: Imagining new uses for information—giving old ideas new purpose by combining ideas that seem to be totally unrelated.

Match quality: A term that describes the amount of fit between the work or activity someone does and who they are—how their abilities match up with what they like.

Molecular biochemist: A scientist who studies chemical processes in living organisms at a molecular level.

Muscular dystrophy: A genetic disease that causes muscles to become increasingly weaker.

Outsider art: Art created by artists who are typically self-taught or who have not received formal training.

Sampling period: A time of trying out many different things.

Spacing: Also known as distributed practice, leaving time between practice sessions for the same material.

Ten-thousand-hours idea: The idea that in order to develop a skill and become an expert at it, the only thing that matters is the number of hours you devote to practicing it.

Varied or mixed practice: Practicing different types of problems, allowing students to apply what they've learned to other areas.

Withered technology: Tech that is old enough to be extremely well understood and easily available.

Acknowledgments

I view book writing in the same way I used to view racing the 800-meters when I was in high school and college—brutal in the middle, but always a learning experience, and extremely rewarding in the end. And as Part 2 of this book insists: learning is supposed to be hard! Writing this book was hard, but I learned so much. First, I'd like to thank Catherine Frank for her caring and wonderful work on this adaptation. Having a book adapted for young readers was a new experience for me, and I'm extremely grateful to have been in such deft hands. I'd also like to thank the team at Viking (especially editor Kelsey Murphy) and the team at Riverhead who worked on the original version of *Range* (especially editor Courtney Young). Books may be old technology, but to me they are still the same magical little puzzle boxes of knowledge I fell in love with as a kid, and I feel incredibly lucky to have worked with two of the greatest publishing imprints in the history of the planet.

Thank you to my agent, Chris Parris-Lamb, for always listening patiently and responding thoughtfully to my ideas, even (or especially) when those ideas are so barely formed that I'm not even sure yet what I'm trying to say. That's the most important time to have a friendly (but critical) conversation partner.

Thanks to fellow author and friend Malcolm Gladwell. The first time we met was in 2014 at the MIT Sloan Sports Analytics Conference for a debate about early specialization and the ten-thousand-hours rule. (It's on YouTube.) It turned into a great discussion, and we both took new thoughts home. He invited me for a run the following day, and then again, and we got to talking (only during warm-up) about that whole "Roger versus Tiger" idea. I didn't know it at the time, but that was the beginning of *Range*.

A special and bittersweet thank-you to three of my intellectual heroes—Robin Hogarth, Daniel Kahneman, and Frances Hesselbein—who shared their time and wisdom when I was working on the original version of this book, and who have since passed away (at the ages of 81, 90, and 107, respectively). I and many others miss them, and I'm eternally grateful to have had the chance to pepper them with questions.

Thank you to my family, and especially my niece, Sigalit.

And finally, Andre: my very own, very young reader. I hope it makes you proud to hold this book.

Index

Index